Formation of the Modern State

Middle East Studies Beyond Dominant Paradigms
Peter Gran, *Series Editor*

Other titles in Middle East Studies Beyond Dominant Paradigms

Formation of the Modern State

The Ottoman Empire,
Sixteenth to Eighteenth Centuries

SECOND EDITION

Rifa'at 'Ali Abou-El-Haj

 Syracuse University Press

Copyright © 2005 by Syracuse University Press
Syracuse, New York 13244–5290
All Rights Reserved

Second Edition 2005
First Syracuse University Press Edition 2005
12 13 14 15 16   6 5 4 3 2

Previously published by the State University of New York Press, Albany, in 1991.
The afterword was previously published, except for small modifications herein, in
the *Andreas Tietze Festschrift* (Prague: Enigma Corp., 1994), 2–18. Reprinted by
arrangement with the author.

∞ The paper used in this publication meets the minimum requirements
of the American National Standard for Information Sciences—Permanence
of Paper for Printed Library Materials, ANSI Z39.48-1992.

For a listing of books published and distributed by Syracuse University Press,
visit our website at SyracuseUniversityPress.syr.edu.

ISBN: 978-0-8156-3085-2

Library of Congress Cataloging-in-Publication Data
Abou-El-Haj, Rifa'at Ali.
Formation of the modern state : the Ottoman Empire, sixteenth to eighteenth
centuries / Rifa'at Ali Abou-El-Haj.— 2nd ed.
p. cm.
Includes bibliographical references and index.
ISBN 0–8156–3085–9 (pbk. : alk. paper)
1. Turkey—History—1453–1683. 2. Turkey—History—1683–1829. I. Title.
DR511.A26 2005
956'.0152—dc22   2005018279

Manufactured in the United States of America

This volume is dedicated to

my rufaqa' *in* Halqat al-'Arbi'a
(Wednesday Study Group of Los Angeles)

Mahmood Ibrahim

Abdul-mola al-Horeir

Mahmud Abuswa

Dina Riziq Khoury

Hala Munthir Fattah

Edward Mitchell

and to the youngest rafiq
Ramkrishna Mukherjee
on his seventy-second birthday

Rifaʻat ʻAli Abou-El-Haj received his Ph.D. from Princeton University and taught as professor of modern European and Near Eastern history at California State University, Long Beach before taking up his current position as professor of modern Near East and European history at the State University of New York at Binghamton. In addition to writing numerous journal articles and book reviews, he is the author of *The Rebellion of 1703 and the Structure of Ottoman Politics* (1984) and coeditor, with I. Bierman and D. Preziosi, of *Ottoman Power and Urban Structure* (1992).

Contents

Preface to the Second Edition

This book represents empirical work based on primary sources and was written with a conscious theoretical bent. Its primary subject is the middle period of Ottoman history, which stands on its own as a discrete and separate phase between the early period of foundation and consolidation and the latter one of "reform" and "modernization." Departing from the conventional historiography, I contend that transformations in the middle period can be demonstrated even when examined principally through Ottoman sources. Such transformations were generated internally, driven by the dynamic needs of certain groups in Ottoman society, rather than by the need to accomodate external pressures.

My training in European history has influenced the historical analogies that informed my understanding of Ottoman historical processes in early modern times. Thanks to Vinay Bahl and Ramkrishna Mukherjee, I have come to think that cogent arguments can be made for drawing historical analogies with the societies of China and the Mugal empire in India during the same period. To address these views, I have added a sequel to this second edition of my book.* I urge readers to entertain further the social rami-

*First published as "Theorizing in Historical Writing: Ottoman Society in the Middle Period," in *Festschrift fur Andreas Tietze,* ed. Ingeborg Baladauf and Suraiya Faroqhi (Prague: Engima Corp., 1994).

fications of comparative studies for the middle Ottoman period.

In the process of thinking through and writing this book, my most productive discussions were with a group of historians informally known as the Wednesday Study Circle, whose contributions I once again acknowledge here. Since the publication of the first edition of this book, I have been inspired by a new generation of young colleagues at the State University of New York at Binghamton: Elif Aksit, Nadir Ozbek, Malek Abisaab, and Cengiz Kirli. Cengiz Kirli in particular admonished me through his own students to pursue the course of scholarship represented by this work. I received the same encouragement from my young colleagues at Princeton: Baki Tezcan, Janet Klein, Christine Philliou, Ipek Yosmaoglu-Taylor, Thomas Papademetriou, Mustafa Aksakal, and Yossef Rapoport.

To my friends and colleagues Ali Ahmida, Peter Gran, Heath Lowry, and Donald Quataert, I wish to express my gratitude for their steady encouragement and support of my work over many years. I am also grateful to Mary Selden Evans of Syracuse University Press for her enthusiastic support for the publication of this second edition of the book.

Finally, I wish to honor the late Andreas Tietze, not only for his generous sharing of scholarship, but for his generous friendship.

RIFA'AT 'ALI ABOU-EL-HAJ
STATE UNIVERSITY OF NEW YORK AT BINGHAMTON
2005

Preface

The study presented here fits into the short but distinguished critical tradition in Middle Eastern history that is associated with names such as Edward Said and Maxime Rodinson. Attempts at critical revaluation are particularly rare in Ottoman history, where well-established paradigms, which will admit some modification but not significant challenge, continue to dominate the field. To name but one example: Ottoman state and society appear in the secondary literature largely as objectively known realities that in essence do not even change over time. Within the confines of this paradigm, the description of Ottoman state and society can be elaborated with respect to details, but the basic configuration of these constructs is known, either from the major historians of the period or else from archival documents. So naive and prosaic a view of reality is, to say the least, astounding, since few readers of twentieth century novels or viewers of modern films would be prepared to see reality in such a light: thus, for example, Akira Kurosawa's film "Rashomon" is based on the assumption that of even a simple event, there will be as many accounts as there are participants, and nobody, not even the dead, will refrain from presenting him/herself in the best possible light. However, in Ottoman studies, we are very willing to forget that everybody, even the historian in his study or the bureaucrat in his office, has an axe to grind, and we are equally reluctant to investigate what kind of an axe that might be.

The bureaucrat in his office is a figure to whom we ascribe an inhuman authority; usually we are more than content to have deciphered the text which his efforts have made available to us, while the less obvious reasons and context for the composition of that document rarely form part of our scholarly agenda. There are other less technical reasons for our reluctance to analyze as well as to describe. After all, our own lives continue to take place within the framework of a national state, and this framework dominates the thinking of even those historians who understand themselves as dealing with the history of large-scale regions or of the globe as a whole. As a result, we have difficulty conceptualizing the manner in which people thought about politics, who lived within a political system that was definitely not the national state. Although on a theoretical level we are quite aware of the difference, in practice we persistently and insidiously slip back into judgments and interpretations which make sense only within the framework of a centralized bureaucratic state. Thus, our often very deficient evaluation of Ottoman documents and the reasons for their composition is due to more than simple negligence, and it is one of the major merits of this study to make this fact very visible.

Moreover, to return to Kurosawa's film and the image of reality projected therein, the most probable account of the central event in the film is placed into the mouth of a character of very little standing, a poor peasant, a lonely woodcutter who, when the occasion presents itself, will not shy away from occasional thievery. Not a commendable character and certainly not particularly credible in a court of law. But the particular axe he has to grind, namely to protect himself from an indictment for thievery, does not necessarily prevent him from observing the crime, which constitutes the center of the story, and rendering an account of who is aggressor and who is victim. Thus, the message of Kurosawa's film may be seen in a challenge to the viewer, namely to go beyond bureaucratic and courtroom criteria, and to judge the varying accounts upon their logical and psychological merits. In similar fashions, the study presented here challenges the reader to go beyond simplistic and bureaucratic criteria when evaluating documentary material. Certainly, such a procedure increases the risk of error; but it is also possible that to risk making even major mistakes of interpretation, and to learn from such mistakes may be more useful to the progress of our discipline than a continuing uncritical accumulation of facts and data.

To a reader who is not part of the world of university politics inhabited by historians of the Middle East in the 1980s and 1990s, many of the basic propositions contained in the present study may seem reasonable but not sensational. That Ottoman history should be taken seriously as a branch of history, that internal dynamics within Ottoman society should be studied in all their ramifications and that mechanistic models of cultural borrowing be avoided, these are all proposals which by themselves appear sensible and not really controversial. More than forty years after the death of Marc Bloch, it is hardly a novelty to call for a comparative approach in order to determine the place of the Ottoman Empire in world history. On the other hand, such relatively innocuous statements may stop being innocuous when one considers the context in which they are made. Analogies readily come to mind. The modern observer may view some of the statements so hotly defended by medieval theologians as part of theoretical quarrels among specialists. Even so, however, we know that at the time when these statements were debated, careers were made and broken according to positions taken during these disputes. One may also cite a more recent example: when in the early 1960s, a German professor published a book stating that the political leaders of Wilhelmian Germany and Habsburg Austria had consciously assumed the risk of war and so had not been merely "overtaken by events," he was saying something inherently probable. It is difficult to assume that any high-ranking politician in any of the major states of the period

was unaware of the risks being taken during the crucial
weeks that preceded August 1914. Yet the hostile reception
that this study provoked shows that, in the German academic environment of that time, the claims made in this
book were the very opposite of trivial. Something similar
may well have happened in the present study; sometimes
it may seem that the violence with which a certain statement is made is somewhat out of proportion to the comparatively innocuous character of the statement itself. But
this fact is in itself indicative of the academic environment which we have created and within which, in the absence of any other, we must operate. In environments in
which "acoustic barriers" have been accepted, even fairly
moderate and reasonable statements can only be made
when the speaker has gathered energy to confront the established views of his/her academic peers, and normally
this energy is accumulated in the form of anger. Most of
us, to be sure, react instinctively with mistrust to words
spoken in anger; but perhaps this mistrust should be only
as great, and no greater, than our mistrust of many established wisdoms accepted by ourselves and most of our
colleagues.

Regarded from a different angle, the study presented
here may be seen as an invitation to study Ottoman history as real history, that is to cope with the complexities
of sources and their interpretation in the manner normally
practiced by medieval or modern historians. This does not
mean that concepts and procedures can be transferred
without further ado from one major cultural area to the
next. After all, the assumption that such a transfer is possible, or even easy, lies at the bottom of much shallow historiography of the nineteenth and twentieth centuries, and
one of the major gains that we have derived from the intensive study of texts in Arabic, Persian, and Turkish is
the realization that basic cultural assumptions are not
necessarily the same in Renaissance Europe and the Middle East of the same period. As an example of the analyti-
cal dangers into which rapid comparison might lead, we
may recall the approval with which the sixteenth century

ambassador Ogier Ghiselin de Busbueq noted that high-level Ottoman officials derived their status from the fact that they were servitors of the sultan rather than members of an hereditary nobility. This observation is partly rooted in European fascination with the servile. The servile legal status of many members of the Ottoman elite, in which Western observers found an explanation for the efficacy of what they saw as Ottoman absolutism; and the power of the myth of the "slave state" has tended to obscure operative differences as well as similarities. To high-level Habsburg officials, service to the Emperor was, of course, equally a source of prestige, but never to the degree prevalent in the sixteenth century Ottoman Empire. After all, members of European noble houses often possessed resources not directly under the control of the local ruler, while Ottoman dignitaries held everything they possessed by the grace of the sultan. To the extent that this difference is confirmed by other sources, it is certainly a feature worth recording and analyzing. All historical analysis is valid only to the extent that close attention is paid to differences between different political and cultural systems.

On the other hand, this should not be taken to mean that Ottoman and Middle Eastern history and European history of the medieval and early modern period are utterly incommensurable. Quite to the contrary, after studying a political, cultural, or economic system by itself and isolating its peculiar dynamics, the next step on the historian's agenda is to figure out how this system compares with other systems in different geographical and historical settings. Ottoman history, and this is one of the major points made in the study introduced here, shares certain features with the early modern history of Europe. This is not really surprising, given the fact that we are concerned with economies based upon agriculture, and with a technology that down to the second half of the eighteenth century was at least broadly comparable. But similarities go beyond what is inherent in the immediate conditions of work. Thus, for example, Venice and the Ottoman Empire used comparable techniques to regulate the grain trade and make sure that large cities were fed even in years of poor harvests, and official attempts in the seventeenth century to deal with irregular soldiers and mercenaries show marked similarities in the Italian and the Ottoman contexts.

Given these circumstances, it makes sense to compare not only economic structures, but also notions of rulership, limitations upon the exercise of political power, attitudes vis-a-vis trade and manual labor, and other matters directly relevant to political life. The present study incorporates a variety of attempts at such cross-cultural comparison, some of them explicit and others implicit. In fact, the title of this study, *Formation of the Modern State: the Ottoman Empire, Sixteenth to Eighteenth Centuries,* is a topic that can scarcely be approached in any other way; without a knowledge of the nature of other types of state (medieval or early modern European, Chinese, Mughal, or whatever), it is scarcely possible to discern anything about the specific nature of the Ottoman state.

If the Ottoman state is thus recognized to be one of a group of "early modern" states, the next step is to establish the stages through which it passed in the course of its historical trajectory, and the points in time at which this state experienced particularly intensive processes of transformation. Professor Abou-El-Haj has identified the seventeenth century as such a period, and he suggests as the basis for this transformation the appropriation as quasi-private property by wealthy Istanbul families and wealthy provincials of much land previously controlled by the state. Through such appropriations, even former servitors of Ottoman governors might acquire a base for political power, and even if such properties were not immune from intervention on the part of the Ottoman state, they were at least very likely to remain in the hands of the same family for the span of several generations. To what extent the power of the Empire's magnates was based upon this change in the system of landholding, and to what extent upon their control of the process of tax extraction, is a question not yet resolved, and for the resolution of this problem we need detailed studies, which at present we do not possess. But debates about the reasons and shape of the Ottoman state's seventeenth century transformation, while important and interesting in themselves, are not really the topic of the study presented here. What is at stake, rather, is the notion that the Ottoman state possessed a dynamic of its own that was connected with changes in the underlying society and not simply with the impact of European states and merchants, as is still often enough assumed even in specialist literature. And beyond lies the notion that we are dealing with intelligible and analyzable processes accessible to reasoning and explanation, and not with more or less mysterious events that can be described and not really understood.

This attempt to make Ottoman history into an object of analysis, and the people who in their time made Ottoman history into historical subjects in their own right, is again an undertaking which may seem noncontroversial and even anodine. When confronted with such a project in the abstract, scarcely an historian would deny that an attempt of this sort is worth undertaking. But in everyday life, such a project is more difficult to follow through than might appear at first glance. One way of documenting one's intention to embark on such a course is generally a change in terminology: in the Ottoman case as well as that of seventeenth century Spain, it is the notion of decline which has been challenged. Professor Abou-El-Haj's study also takes issue with the biologistic implications of the term "decline," and of the lack of scope for political action that this image implies. Moreover, the most insidious aspect of such images is probably that everyone assumes that he/she knows what is meant by this term, so that its widespread application preempts all serious research into the processes that were actually going on in the Ottoman Empire of the sixteenth or seventeenth century.

However, even abandoning the term "decline," and replacing it by a more neutral term such as "transformation," does not resolve the problem. Terms are, after all, nothing more than convenient labels, and ultimately the historian proves him/herself not by the labels used, but by the concrete analyses undertaken. Thus, it might be considered one of the merits of this study that the author is fairly eclectic in his use of terms, and on the whole concentrates on issues and not on labels.

At the core of Professor Abou-El-Haj's thinking lies the Ottoman state. This concern with the state fits into a current of thinking which has become characteristic of European historians during the last ten years or so. Admittedly many of the greatest practitioners of social and economic history, such as Marc Bloch or perhaps even Fernand Braudel, throughout their work had never left the state out of consideration. But at the same time, one school of thought among social and economic historians in both France and England has been inclined to focus on production and distribution patterns, and relegate the state to the background. Given the fact that old style political history had concerned itself with the state to the practical exclusion of anything else, even such an extreme reaction appears comprehensible. However, with the later seventies, it was discovered that the state grew and transformed itself in a measurable manner which could be expressed in tables and graphs, just as any economic conjuncture. Moreover, economic historians rediscovered the well-known fact that much of economic history was very strongly determined by the actions of the state. Given these circumstances, we observe a marked trend toward "bringing the state back in," although many of the practitioners of the "new" political history rather resemble economic and social historians in their working procedures.

Ottoman history, on the other hand, has followed a different trajectory. Social and economic history has developed fairly vigorously, on the whole showing more vitality than traditional political history. However, given the fact that the masses of Ottoman archival documentation are almost all a product of the state and particularly the financial bureaucracy, the affinity between socioeconomic and political history has always remained quite close. In fact,

Ottoman socioeconomic history, like old-fashioned European political history, has concerned itself with the Ottoman state almost to the exclusion of anything else. Viewed from this angle, Professor Abou-El-Haj's work on the Ottoman state responds to a problematique which is current in both early modern European and Ottoman history, and perhaps by this very fact demonstrates that there is an urgency for the kind of comparative approach which he advocates in this study.

SURAIYA FAROQHI, LUDWIG-MAXIMILIANS UNIVERSITÄT MÜNCHEN
CORNELL FLEISCHER, WASHINGTON UNIVERSITY, ST. LOUIS

Acknowledgments

On three occasions I explored some aspects of the issues raised in this study: the Vienna CIEPO (1982), the Faculty Seminar, Center for Near Eastern Studies, University of California, Los Angeles (1983), and the Cambridge (U.K.) CIEPO (1984). I am grateful to my friends and colleagues who have commented on different versions of this study: Barbara Abou-El-Haj, Samira Abu El-Haj, Engin Akarli, Talal Asad, Kenneth Cuno, Peter Gran, Afaf Lutfi al-Sayyid Marsot, Edward Mitchell, Ilber Ortayli, Andreas Tietze, Speros Vryonis, Jr., and Richard Wilde. Approaching this study as a joint venture, Suraiya Faroqhi and Cornell Fleischer took large blocks of their time to go over the manuscript and have been valuable critics. Finally, I wish to thank the four anonymous readers of the manuscript of this book for their cogent suggestions. Wherever I could, I incorporated materials in the footnotes to follow some of their suggestions.

I am especially grateful to my friend Marina Preussner who did copy editing and editorial work on the manuscript of this study. Whatever errors remain are my total responsibility.

Partial support for writing this monograph was provided by the California State University, Long Beach, and the Institute for Turkish Studies.

Note on Transliteration

Throughout, where feasible and appropriate, modern Turkish transliteration of Ottoman Turkish has been used. For Arabic texts a modified *Encyclopedia of Islam* system of transliteration was followed. In the text I used 'Ali to represent 'Aali.

The Study

If history is a science, it should be possible to treat and analyze Ottoman history according to criteria commensurate with those that have been developed in studying the history of other areas. Such an approach should facilitate the entry of Ottoman history into the discourse of comparative history, thereby allowing communication across ethnic, national, civilizational, and continental divides. Global communication of this kind in turn should allow one to bridge the gap that today separates historians and social scientists, most particularly historically oriented sociologists and anthropologists. Many historians see themselves, and consequently are seen by others, as being concerned mainly with the study of the particular, the unique, and the nonrepetitive. This type of orientation, even though much reduced in the last fifty years or so, still can be observed even among historians of Europe.[1] In Middle Eastern history, and particularly in Ottoman history, where research moves at a much slower pace, these attitudes are very prevalent. As a result, present day historiography of the Ottoman Empire continues to emphasize the peculiarities, oddities, and particularism of Ottoman history and civilization. The present study is intended as a plea for a reversal of this trend.

1

I.

A general look at the present state of historiography concerning the Ottoman Empire soon makes it apparent that the scholarly cost of particularism has been high, because the emphasis on the incomparability and incommensurability of Ottoman history with other histories has narrowed our perspective and has given rise to many distortions. Ottoman historians are often inclined to treat phenomena that occur throughout the world in vastly different states and cultures, such as, for instance, tax farming, as if they were the outcome of purely conjunctural factors affecting the Ottoman Empire and the Ottoman Empire alone. Ottoman specialists have emphasized the "differentness" of their chosen subject to such an extent that a dialogue with neighboring historical disciplines has become difficult if not impossible. We have made our field into such an esoteric one that most of the time other researchers cannot fathom what we are trying to do. This difficulty brings another in its wake, and to my mind, this second problem is even more serious, from a scientific point of view. Our tendency to isolate ourselves in a small esoteric group has made it impossible to develop any sustained scholarly interchange even within the broader field of Near Eastern studies. As a result, most scholars in Ottoman history proceed in a most uncritical fashion when they read one another's work. In addition, the dearth of scholarly communication and exchange puts us all too often in the position of duplicating one another's work, with all the waste of time and energy that this involves.

It must be admitted also that most studies in the wider Near Eastern field are written from a noncomparative point of view. This state of affairs makes it impossible for the researcher to carry on any discourse with other specialists. At a future occasion I hope to address the question of why there is hardly any scholarly dialogue (across specialists' lines) between Near Eastern historians and specialists in other areas.

Scholarly particularism not only misleads Ottomanists

but also compounds the dilemma of those nonspecialists who are anxious to write comparative history that includes the Ottomans in their studies. A noteworthy example is Perry Anderson, who in a book focused on European absolutist states, has included a chapter on the Ottoman Empire.[2] Basing himself upon the standard secondary literature, Anderson underlines what he regards as the unique character of the European historic trajectory by stressing the features in which the Ottoman Empire differed from Europe. Since moreover he places a high value upon the political and social results of the historical processes he discerns in early modern Europe, he regards Ottoman history as not only different, but also as inferior. But at the same time Anderson genuinely wishes to tackle Ottoman history from a progressive perspective. Thereby his treatment adds some further complications for those Ottoman historians who attempt to develop counterpositions against the dominant conservative paradigm. More than a few established Ottoman historians, with their emphasis on the Empire's decline and modernization, have imposed a perspective in which Ottoman state and society appear both different from and inferior to their European counterparts. Those Ottoman historians who are working toward a revision of these unscientific views now need to grapple not only with the more old-fashioned, modernization-oriented, and European-centered paradigm, but also with the progressive variant proposed by Anderson.

For what is ostensibly a historical treatment, Anderson starts with some curious assumptions, for example, the notion that the Ottomans represented a less developed civilizational formation than that found in Europe.[3] This claim sets the tone for his study of Ottoman history in the early modern period. Anderson considers the Ottoman state to be an intrusion on the European continent, albeit an intrusion that lasted for five hundred years. He evaluates this intrusion as one that created problems "to unitary histories of the continent," since the Ottomans were never "naturalized into (Europe's) social or political system"(p. 397).

Anderson sets up a typically Eurocentric answer to the question why the Ottoman Empire is important in world history, an answer he must have had in the back of his mind even as he started to consider Ottoman history. To state the matter in his own words: "In fact, the long and intimate presence on European soil of a social formation and state structure in such contrast with the prevalent pattern of the continent, provides an apposite measure against which to assess the historical specificity of European society before the advent of industrial capitalism."[4] Anderson goes further, picking up the traditional Orientalist theme of Ottoman decline and attributing it to the usual external causes: "The long-term decline of the Ottoman Empire was determined by the military and economic superiority of Absolutist Europe."[5] He reduces Ottoman state and society to a kind of backdrop to the unfolding drama of world history, which in his view is equated with the history of the principal European states.

It should be pointed out in Anderson's defense that he is not a specialist on early modern Ottoman history, and that he has arrived at his simplistic and narrow explanations of Ottoman affairs by faithfully following the available secondary literature. As a consequence, he winds up doing something that was not necessarily part of his original intention, namely, reinforcing regressive paradigms through the reintroduction, in what seems to be totally new garb, of the same old cliched interpretations of Ottoman history. He develops his own explanations for the internal dynamics of such historically evolved practices as the shift from charismatic leadership to leadership based on a collective ruling class, but in so doing, he simply repeats the standard explanations. To name but one example, he views the introduction of the royal cage, or *kafes*, in the following manner:

"In the seventeenth century, the calibre of the imperial rulers—whose despotic authority had hitherto generally been exercised with considerable ability—collapsed because of a new succession system." (From now on, the throne passed to the eldest surviving male of the Osmanli line.)" Princes were placed in " . . . damascened dungeons virtually designed to produce pathological imbalance or imbecility. Such Sultans were in no position to control or check the steady deterioration of the State system beneath them. It was in this epoch that clericalist manoeuvres by the Sheikh-ul-Islam started to encroach on the system of political decision, which became steadily more venal and unstable."[6]

This passage contains several misunderstandings, and to discuss them *in extenso* would lead the reader far away from the present topic. Suffice it to say that seventeenth century Ottoman rulers ruled in only a limited sense; their presence was necessary so that bureaucratic commands could be appropriately legitimized. Mehmed IV (1648–1687) for example, was a child during a considerable part of his reign, yet the state apparatus functioned adequately without him. The sultans of the seventeenth century did participate in politics, and a major political mistake could, and occasionally did, cost them their throne. But basically, the Empire was governed by bureaucrats who were based in the palace or the grand vezir's office, and the major officeholders used their households as a means for the recruitment and training of new personnel. In this context, the madness of Deli Ibrahim (1640–1648) was a minor matter, and to take the personality defects of some rulers as a starting point for dealing with the question of Ottoman decline represents a grave misunderstanding. It must be admitted, however, that similar misconceptions still dominate twentieth century Ottoman historiography, and a specialist on early modern Europe, even one who might wish to challenge the current paradigm, would have great difficulty in locating the appropriate secondary literature.

Given this background of reproduced and perpetuated misconceptions, it is not surprising that specialists on Ottoman affairs on both sides of the Atlantic should frequently complain that other historians are indifferent to engaging Ottoman historians in any kind of dialogue on any aspect of their subject. Those few who do, like Anderson, focus on the odd, the unique, and the peculiar characteristics of Ottoman state and society. It is these particular features that seem to attract attention, rather than those which the Ottoman Empire shared with other societies, and which, therefore, are accessible to broader comparison.[7]

As a way out of this impasse, I would suggest replacing the old notion that Ottoman state and society were essentially unique with the proposition that Ottoman history is comparable and commensurable with other histories. I would go even further and say that as far as seventeenth century history is concerned, there are profound correspondences between the Ottoman Empire and Europe, and these parallels suggest some of the issues that Ottoman historians might pursue in reassessing Ottoman history. Two themes in particular stand out in the recent European historiography of the seventeenth century: one focuses on the possibility of an economic and social revolution, and the other is concerned with the changing character of the state. Historians have long debated whether or not a given country experienced a major revolution or a series of social and economic crises which amounted to a revolution. The issues raised have led to sustained debates on the meaning of the term revolution in a preindustrial context: can one assume, for example, that during the seventeenth century English revolution wealthier or rising gentry generally sided with the powers that be against the rebels, or was enrichment or impoverishment irrelevant in this context?[8] Or in another example, from seventeenth century France: were the rural rebellions that shook the country motivated by peasant resentment against the dominant classes, or should they be considered as provincial movements, headed by the gentry and directed against the centralizing tendencies of the emerging early modern state?[9]

Although the debate on seventeenth century revolutions is intimately connected with a discussion of the early modern state, some historians approach the nature of the state in a more direct manner. They wonder whether the state, in its precapitalist formation, should be studied as an autonomous entity separate from its class base, or whether it is no more and no less than an extension of the ruling class. Anyone studying the early modern European state should consider at the very least the following alternative approaches. (1) The state is class-based and functions to all intents and purposes as an extension of the ruling class; (2) The state is class-based but autonomous; that is, while it represents the interests of the ruling class as a whole, the interests of subsections within the ruling class may be sacrificed "for the good of society," and left with no alternative but to comply; (3) The state is part of the ruling class, but for its own advantage forges alliances with local or regional elites; (4) The state is autonomous and not based upon any particular class; to the contrary, the officials serving the state perceive themselves as transcending class divisions in the area they govern. The development in Europe of absolutist monarchies striving toward an early modern type of centralization can be understood as one stage in the process whereby the state gained increasing autonomy. Here we may have an example of the tendency toward a progressive separation between the state and the ruling class.[10]

The advance in historiographical thinking found in recent work on seventeenth-century European history is based upon a body of advanced scholarship produced over the last quarter of a century. Without this rich scholarship and historiography, the debate over state or society and the "revolution" of the seventeenth century would have remained at the abstract and theoretical level. While similar debates concerning state, society, and political transformations ought to be taking place for the Ottoman realm as well, research on these topics is very limited indeed. Worldwide, there are fewer than fifty historians engaged in the study of Ottoman society of the sixteenth and seventeenth centuries. Since there is so little scholarly literature available, those Ottoman historians who do work on this period are obliged to be far more speculative than their European counterparts when introducing and discussing revisionist interpretations.[11]

Within Ottoman historiography, the treatment of the state (and of society) has played an especially critical role in setting the parameters of nearly all the research that has been carried out to date for all periods of Ottoman history. In particular, assumptions guiding scholarly research on the early modern and modern Ottoman periods accord a prominent place to the state as an institution, especially with regard to its bureaucracy and administrative practices.

In twentieth century scholarly writing on Ottoman affairs, the concept, the institution, and the nature of the state have been treated as if, regardless of the passage of time, the state had remained essentially the same. The term state possesses the same connotations and denotations throughout the entire course of Ottoman history, and no differentiation is drawn between the early modern period (which for the purposes of this study is the fourteenth through the seventeenth century) and the modern period (which encompasses the eighteenth and the nineteenth centuries). Such simplification is bad enough in itself; but to compound the problem, nearly all the scholarly literature I have reviewed is premised on the unspoken, perhaps even unconscious, assumption that the modern standards of the nation-state constitute the unchallenged norm by which to assess early modern political life. Determinations are made without regard for any historical transformations from early modern times to the fully developed and virtually autonomous modern institution. The scholarly literature measures the early modern Ottoman state by such modern sociologically evolved standards as merit, public service, equity, and rationalized practices—the very same standards that modern, and specifically twentieth century social science has reserved for evaluating the efficacy of the modern nation-state.

This anachronistic treatment first of all leads to a displacement of emphasis and to misconceptions in the study of Ottoman society and state. Second, because of the misappropriation of categories used in historical analysis, Ottoman society is treated by a more subjective standard than its early modern counterparts in Europe. For example, corruption with respect to appointments to public office was a regular occurrence in England during the eighteenth century, and specialists dealing with this area treat the phenomenon of corruption as a topic for legitimate scholarly analysis.[12] Yet when treating the equivalent feature in Ottoman state and society historians do not analyze corruption—they simply condemn it. Admittedly, a rationale for approaching "early modern" corruption against modern sociological standards comes readily to mind, since some of the Ottoman authors of the later sixteenth and seventeenth centuries also take an abstract and moralistic approach when inveighing against corruption. But historians pride themselves on the critical use they make of the available sources. Had Ottoman authors not been concerned with corruption, it would still be necessary to try to find out whether the "standard" member of the Ottoman ruling class saw his relationship to the available fiscal resources in the same manner, say, as did a virulent critic of the Ottoman establishment such as the sixteenth century writer Mustafa 'Ali. In other words, only after an investigation of the facts has been made can one compare the understanding of corruption such as may have existed in the second half of the sixteenth century with the conception that prevails today, after the nation-state has had time to take root.[13]

An uncritical reading of the Ottoman sources, with their emphasis upon bureaucratic merit, predisposes the researcher to regard the modern nation-state with its meritocratic bureaucracy as a paradigm applicable to the study of the early modern period as well. As a consequence, social and economic transformations in the Ottoman sixteenth and seventeenth centuries are either totally ignored, or are forced into the nation-state framework of analysis. This approach should not be regarded simply as an intellectual error, for value judgments are equally at play. Evaluating the early modern Ottoman state according to criteria designed for the modern nation-state tends to reinforce a comfortable feeling of superiority in scholars from Europe and America, a state of mind which, as already seen, may sometimes be found even among those scholars who try to view history in a progressive perspective. The unhistorical character of such attempts becomes even more obvious when one examines some of the underlying assumptions. Chief among these is the misapprehension that prior to the seventeenth century the Ottoman state was a centralized, efficient, and rational public entity, unique in the period during which it flourished. The presumption follows that by the seventeenth century the Ottoman state had lost whatever unique features it had once possessed and had begun to disintegrate. The process of disintegration is presumed to have started late in the sixteenth century. Another misconception is that such features as the rationalism and public service that characterize the modern state are totally unprecedented in Ottoman history. Therefore, with the dawning of modern times, the nation-state was presumably imposed on the underlying Ottoman society by the ruling elite. This model makes it unnecessary to examine the history of the previous three hundred years, which is apparently irrelevant to the experiences of the nineteenth and twentieth centuries. Further, socioeconomic transformations are seen primarily in terms of how they affect the functioning of the state. Little attention is paid to the possibility that the state may in turn reflect transformations in economy and society. Behind these distortions in interpretation and understanding lies a literalist and unreflective reading of Ottoman sources, as shall be discussed below.

To date, enough evidence has been accumulated to allow historians to begin considering whether the "classical" themes of seventeenth century European history are appropriate to Ottoman history as well. In European history, an economic and social revolution was postulated and questions were raised on whether the revolution was of a nature to transform the state. What do these themes teach about the relationship between Ottoman social and economic structures on the one hand, and the political superstructure on the other? When comparative approaches to Ottoman history have become more developed and more sophisticated, it will be possible to determine whether the links between the political and socioeconomic structures in the Ottoman Empire were similar to

those in Europe, or whether the relationship between a social and economic revolution and the transformation of
the state differed in certain respects from one polity to the
other. In the long run, comparisons of this kind may carry
historians beyond the confines of Europe and the Middle
East; it would be particularly instructive to study the seventeenth century peasant rebellions of China from such a
comparative context. Whether or not a seventeenth century transformation of the Ottoman state took place is a
question of interest not only by and of itself, but also one
that allows the historian to tie in Ottoman history with
world history.

II.

Given the present dearth in knowledge, the Ottoman
problems of the seventeenth century constitute too large a
task to be tackled by a single researcher. At this stage of
inquiry, the question that must be raised is simply why
there were major social and economic upheavals at this
particular time. Any attempt to explain these upheavals
shows that they form part of a pattern, and that Ottomans
and Europeans of the seventeenth century experienced
comparable economic and political dislocations, which
can be regarded as symptoms of a far-reaching transformation. What is most striking, however, is the state of perpetual rebellion in a good number of Ottoman domains
during this period.[14]

The underlying economic issues of the sixteenth and
seventeenth centuries continue to be argued according to
competing theories. Contributions to the debate are articles by Halil Inalcik, Huricihan Islamoglu and Çaglar Keyder, and Huricihan Islamoglu and Suraiya Faroqhi.[15]
Inalcik takes a monetarist view, to the effect that the flood
of New World silver entering the Ottoman domains and
the resulting liquidity crisis of the Ottoman state constitute the primary contributing factor to the disruptions
of the seventeenth century. Inalcik focuses on external

factors, whereas his challengers maintain that the Ottoman socioeconomic structure changed as the result of
modifications in the way land (especially the *miri* or public land) was held. Islamoglu and Keyder and Islamoglu
and Faroqhi regard modification in land tenure patterns as
a result of the impingement of the world market on local
Ottoman resources and marketing networks. While this
last position is the more cogent of the two, one needs to
avoid its implied mechanistic approach. Excessive emphasis on world market conditions accords high priority to external causes for change, and as a result undervalues the
indigenous roots for internal change in Ottoman society in
the sixteenth and most of the seventeenth centuries. Recent studies on Egypt by Kenneth Cuno and on developments in southern Mesopotamia, eastern Arabia, and
southwestern Iran by Hala Munthir Fattah trace the rise of
regional and local markets to well before involvement in
the world market.[16] These studies will be discussed briefly
later; here it needs only be said that a more comprehensive
study of internal changes in the Ottoman Empire of the
seventeenth century will show that they came about as a
result of a complex process involving both internal conditions, and especially later in the period, external factors,
though not necessarily with equal force.

During this period the worsening economic conditions
turned into a crisis, attributable in part to an intense experimentation with taxation aimed at increasing surplus
product and resources for the benefit of the ruling elites.
The intensification of surplus extraction was paralleled by
disruption in the old administrative and political order.

In the earlier period, especially in the fifteenth century
under Sultan Fatih Mehmed, when a consensus of sorts
prevailed among the ruling elite, coercive power to impose
its will was exemplified especially in the way the state extracted taxes from the common people (*reaya*). The consensus appeared concretely in a fairly successful early
modern form of political centralization. At one stage, Ottoman centralization included its own class-bound system
of reward for merit—the rotation of appointments to fiefs

(*timars*)—in addition to easy and frequent appointment to or removal from high office. The ruling class implemented these political moves with confidence. Members of the Ottoman ruling establishment were not excessively concerned whether the reaya would deliver their taxes or not to the next assignee (fief-holder), or object to the appointment of a specific individual to high office, or to the removal of another. For a while the ruling class was united enough and mustered sufficient coercive power to assert its will and discourage local resistance. Late in the sixteenth century, the historian and litterateur Mustafa 'Ali dwells on the ability of the ruling class to enforce its power as special attributes of the strength and gifts once possessed by the Ottoman dynasty.[17]

Another significant manifestation of early modern centralization is illustrated by the effort to "Ottomanize," that is, to codify the provincial regulations known as the *liva kanunnameleri* or *sancak kanunnameleri*. Conformity to these centrally conceived tax regulations was insisted upon "without exceptions."[18] Sixteenth century liva kanunnameleri, especially though not exclusively from the Arab provinces, point to an initial effort at reaffirming most of the provincial regulations and laws which had existed prior to the acquisition of these provinces, whether by conquest or by peaceful annexation. The provincial tax codes were amended or reproduced at intervals throughout the sixteenth century and early part of the seventeenth. After that period the production of codes nearly halted, because the centrally imposed tax regulations were abandoned in most of the Ottoman domains during the seventeenth century. This was a change of some moment, for it indicates a transition from an established, and on the whole, stable system of revenue collection to a situation in which fixed rules no longer obtained, and in which maximization of revenues became the one and only concern. In the scramble for higher revenues, formally enacted tax regulations had become all but irrelevant.

The abandonment of the liva kanunnameleri and the growing pace of tax experimentation should be taken as symptoms of the breakdown of whatever form early modern centralization had taken in the fifteenth and sixteenth centuries. It should therefore also suggest a diminution in the coercive powers of the ruling class in Istanbul. As I have noted elsewhere, important changes were taking place in the composition of the ruling elite, accompanied by the loss of a consensus which up to that time had preserved a balance of power.[19] Eventually, the consequent loss of balance of power led to a more open intra-elite political struggle at the center, manifested by a growing decentralization of authority and an end to the early modern class-bound merit for-service-system. There is no doubt that the struggles within the ruling elite also affected its capacity to collect taxes.

The tax paying Ottoman subjects, especially the peasants among them, did not remain passive spectators of the struggle for revenue collection. Social conflicts surfaced, usually in the form of resistance to the experiments in revenue extraction so frequent at this time. Peasants in early seventeenth century Anatolia built improvised earthworks in the vicinity of their villages, and from the shelter of these strongholds refused to pay their dues. Others invoked the protection of influential figures in Istanbul against rapacious provincial governors and their tax collectors.[20] The peasants' resistance can be explained easily if one considers that the new forms of revenue extraction consisted of variations on a single practice, namely, the privatization of what was once considered public property, and the consequent change in the relationship of the reaya to the land. (Regional exceptions apart, peasants held their land individually, and not in common.) A further observation needs to be made at this point. Whether the Ottoman state extracted taxes mostly in cash or mostly in kind constitutes one of the major issues in the debate on the nature of the Ottoman state within Ottoman historiography. Evidence in the liva kanunnameleri, suggests that even in the beginning of the sixteenth century, this early period, there was a trend in favor of cash extraction. The records also document a de facto shift from product to

cash payment, which the central government was power-
less to prevent, though some liva kanunnameleri, for example the one for Mosul, expressly prohibits demands for
payment in money.[21] A similar prohibition is recorded in a
sixteenth century district court record or *sicillat-i şeriye*
for Jerusalem.[22] We may conclude that from the sixteenth
century onward, the use of money was progressing on the
upper levels of the Ottoman economy, and that timar
holders and other claimants to peasant surpluses reflected
a growing trend. It is probable that peasants were still find-
ing it difficult and burdensome to convert their tax gains
into money, and the prohibitions in some of the liva kanunnameleri probably reflect their protests.

From the seemingly confused and arbitrary practices of
seventeenth century revenue extraction, an overall trend
does in fact emerge. The central government often lost
control over surplus extraction, which resulted in the progressive disappearance of the timar holders, who were government appointees without any power to dictate the
terms of their appointment. Revenue extraction gradually
fell under the control of tax farmers, who were much more
difficult to depose, a state of affairs that had repercussions
on the local level as well. The new style tax collectors operated close to the source of revenue, initially as agents for
the major tax farmers, who bought at auction the right to
collect revenue. The more important tax farmers were
often found among high- and middle-level Istanbul-based
officials. Their agents supervised revenue sources and en-
sured that taxes were delivered promptly, in some instances both to the main tax farmer and directly to the
imperial treasury. The shift from taxation in kind to taxation in cash took place with a commensurate change on
the sociopolitical level, manifested in a transformation in
the composition of the ruling elite at the center and in the
provinces. The process began in the sixteenth century, but
became statistically significant only in the seventeenth.[23]

The interests of the newly emerging tax farmers large
and small demanded that they retain control of taxable resources for reasonably long periods of time. Toward the

end of the seventeenth century, as tax farms were converted from short- and fixed-term forms into a lifelong right for the successful bidder at auction, an organizational mode was found to accommodate the demands of some of the major tax farmers.[24] The lifelong tax farms allowed the more important tax farmers to calculate future income to a much greater extent than had been possible in the past, since yearly installments were low and fixed for the life of the grantee. For example, a tax farmer who had paid the substantial downpayment demanded by the treasury could now look forward to a hitherto unprecedented security of tenure.

Experimentation with revenue extraction reached its peak in the eighteenth century with the extensive practice of *mülk* grants, which converted public lands outright into registered private property. The history of these grants can be traced to grants of freehold property made to "lords of the marches" on the Balkan frontier during the later fourteenth and early fifteenth centuries. Similar grants are known from the second half of the sixteenth century and the beginning years of the seventeenth as well, and contemporary writers such as Mustafa 'Ali and Koçu Bey have commented on them. For the later seventeenth century, I might mention the case of Rami Mehmed Paşa, later to become grand vezir, who early in his career was granted former miri lands as private property. The practice became a great deal more frequent in the eighteenth century than it had been previously; this was also the period during which elite families such as that of the Jalilis of Mosul, for example, were offered *temliknames* which conferred large tracts of public land as private property.

We may assume that the transformations in Ottoman society which started in the sixteenth century continued into the seventeenth.[25] The transformations resulted in numerous and sometimes violent rebellions in the Rumelian and Anatolian countryside. Some rebellions resulted in the granting by the Ottoman administration of provincial dynastic control to successful rebels. As examples

from the seventeenth century, I might mention the Mount
Lebanon rebellion headed by Ma'anoglu and the rising
power of the sherifs in the Hijaz.[26] Interestingly enough,
by the eighteenth century the central state had become so
dependent on the provincial magnates not only for internal security but for protection from external aggression,
that it had to solicit the help of their armed forces in its
quarrels with foreign powers.

Beginning in 1648, the provincial rebellions coincided
at the center with the forcible removal from power of four
sultans, a sequence of events which indicates that elite
configurations at the center were changing also. Some of
the royal depositions were accompanied by violent and
bloody confrontations that parallel the fiscal transformations characteristic of the times, such as for instance, the
several experiments which in 1695 led to the adoption of
malikane tax-farming.

Already in the late 1500s there is evidence that the
peasants were reacting to all the turmoil by abandoning
their homes and their plots. Mustafa 'Ali comments on
this phenomenon when he indicates that thousands of formerly peasant reaya were known to have settled in cities
as artisans. He laments further the consequent double loss
to the treasury, first, of the neglect-of-land tax or *çift-
bozan* dues, which often remained unpaid, and second, because as the fleeing reaya became new artisans they did
not pay the taxes which in more normal times had been
paid by craftsmen and shopkeepers.[27] From Mustafa 'Ali's
treatment it appears as though the reaya voluntarily and
deliberately abandoned the countryside in favor of urban
centers. Koçu Bey discusses the phenomenon from another
perspective. Writing in the first half of the seventeenth
century, he deplores the erosion of barriers that had once
separated the orders or classes of society. He comments on
the fact that in his time it had become difficult to differentiate a tax-paying subject from a member of the governing class, what with the reaya donning the outer garments
of other social orders, riding horses, and carrying firearms

like military men. To this erosion of corporate distinction, Koçu Bey attributes the social rebellions of the time.[28] Other seventeenth century Ottoman chroniclers equally record various instances of social protest. Some protests were directed against changes in the form of landholding, others were the result of transformations in both political and social structures.[29]

In spite of evidence, however, twentieth century researchers have for the most part been reluctant to admit that the social and economic transformations that were taking place throughout the Ottoman Empire in the seventeenth century amounted to a change in social formation. Islamoglu and Keyder insist that in spite of the changes I have outlined, the same social formation continued, albeit in altered forms.[30] One may speculate that Ottoman historians have become so accustomed to thinking of Ottoman state and society as an all but immobile structure that they have great conceptual difficulties in reorienting themselves even when new evidence demonstrates the contrary of mobility. But in the long run, Ottoman historians cannot avoid facing the obvious question: How much change does there have to be before they will admit an overall transformation of state and society?[31]

III.

The nature of Ottoman state and society can be examined by contrasting evidence from the latter part of the sixteenth century with evidence from the late seventeenth. Here it is useful to reintroduce briefly the ongoing debate among historians of seventeenth and eighteenth century Europe. Recent scholarship has explored the issue of the emerging autonomy of the state vis-a-vis the ruling class of the period. One side of the debate suggests that precapitalist (or early modern) state formations are indistinguishable from the ruling classes that dominate them. In the subsequent stages of the debate another focus predominates and researchers discuss whether the separation between state and ruling class and the development of state autonomy were conditioned by the emergence of capitalism. This problem continues to be the subject of heated argument. It may be recalled that there are secondary debates within the larger one, which examine the relative degree of autonomy that the state, in its latter-day evolution, obtains under specific historical conditions. One instance is the rise of Bonapartism as a result of a class struggle in which the power of the ruling class is nearly equal to that which its opponent can muster. Other debates concern the different natures and degrees of early modern and modern processes of centralization.[32]

In Ottoman usage the term for state is *devlet*. Modern historians have almost invariably misunderstood this term to have both the connotation and the denotation of the modern nation-state. Most often their misunderstanding is automatic, for it is difficult to find in the secondary literature a substantial discussion of the concrete changes of the historical phenomenon that the term devlet purports to represent. Andreas Tietze has provided one of the most suggestive definitions of what was meant by devlet in the seventeenth century. In an early discussion of the phenomenon he qualified it as "the decision-making power of the legitimate head of state as well as of those to whom he has delegated this power. The phrase *din u devlet* (religion and state) refers perhaps to the general climate produced by this power in the community under the aspect of perpetuating itself."[33]

That the term devlet as used in the sixteenth and seventeenth centuries carried strong religious connotations is apparent. Apart from the commonly used phrase din u devlet, as one example among many one might refer to the practice of granting pensions to various elderly people, who in recognition of the sultan's bounty were expected to pray for the continuing existence of the state. At the same time, in the day-to-day operation of the Ottoman state, religious legitimation was seldom invoked; quite the contrary, one comes away from Ottoman archival materials with the impression that sixteenth and seventeenth century officials were concerned with the intricacies of implementing policy, less so with the general principles that informed the policies to be implemented. Obviously the tendency by sixteenth and seventeenth century authors to take the devlet for granted does not facilitate the task of the modern historian, who is thereby deprived of the source materials which a more open discussion would have generated. This difficulty may explain the lack, to the present day, of systematic studies on the nature of the early modern Ottoman state and society.

In the absence of secondary materials, it is possible to resort to the analyses of selected sixteenth through eighteenth century authors which give a central place to the operation of the Ottoman state.[34] One useful type of primary sources is the literature of advice to princes, or *nasihatname*. There are also useful historiographical treatises, a good example is Naima's *History*. Both types of sources are naturally distorted by the political partisanship of their authors, but even through this refraction the texts provide glimpses of seventeenth century society and state. Significantly enough, the ostensible impetus for the *nasihat* genre was the guidance of princes in the management of their personal and public affairs (in some periods the two were considered inseparable). There is no such immediately practical aim in Naima's chronicle, but he treats state and society in a polemical preface to a historical account of seventeenth and eighteenth century political events.

Among the *nasihatnames*, Koçu Bey's *Risale*, written in the first half of the seventeenth century, is particularly valuable for the purposes of the present study, for it provides three distinct advantages. First of all, it was composed before 1650 and therefore allows the tracing of some of the social, political, and economic trends that had been set in motion in the sixteenth century. This retrospective aspect of Koçu Bey's work is particularly important because changes occurring in the sixteenth century paved

the ground for the major transformations discernible by
the end of the seventeenth. Among the most obvious examples of changes that took place about 1600 is the gradual phasing out of the timar system, which authors of
Koçu Bey's time still tended to regard as the symbol of Ottoman greatness. Historians in the late twentieth century,
however, view the timar system as indication that the
early Ottoman Empire flourished in an environment in
which coins were rare, and in which firearms were mostly
a matter of artillery. Population growth, the spread of
handguns, the influx of foreign silver, and the aggressive
trading practices of European merchants all combined, in
varying degrees (the exact role of these factors is still hotly
debated), to increase monetary circulation, drive up prices
of essential supplies, and induce the Ottoman administration to gradually substitute tax farming for the timar.
Koçu Bey was highly sensitive to the social consequences
of the prevailing economic and political instability. Since
he and his fellow scholar officials understood the strict
separation between taxpayers and ruling group to be a basic principle of Ottoman political organization, they perceived any blurring of the distinction as an indication of a
severe political crisis.

Another advantage provided by Koçu Bey's treatise is
one of structure. Within the genre, Koçu Bey's work is the
only text that details both what Ottoman society and the
state were like in earlier eras, and what they had become
at the time of his writing. For the earlier years Koçu Bey
sketches a picture of the Ottoman state and society as he
imagined them to have existed at the time of the Empire's
greatest achievements, drawing for his sources on the
rules, regulations, and the etiquette that once had dictated
acceptable behavior for the different classes.

Koçu Bey facilitates the work of the modern researcher
in yet another way, for he provides a fairly comprehensive
view of state and society in his own time, including con
temporary details, specific dates, individuals, and events.
Past and present are linked by his interpretation. From

Koçu Bey's perspective, his own time is characterized by the violation, even the outright breakdown of the practices outlined in the first part of his commentary. His assessment of these changes is expressed in generalizations: his times represent a disruption of the *nizam-i alem* or world order. (An expression found in Ottoman literary and political writings, nizam-i alem both denotes and connotes the Ottoman world.)

It is possible to supplement Koçu Bey's contrasting historical and ideal structures with details from earlier and later examples of the nasihatname genre, keeping in mind that this process may distort and blur somewhat the specificity of each of the examples drawn upon.[36] Starting with the premise that the writings are indeed political tracts that represent a struggle within the ruling elite, I will emphasize the need for a methodology that treats each representative of the genre as the product of specific historical factors. A close analysis of nasihatname texts from Koçu Bey's time can give the researcher a synthetic picture to compare and contrast with the one drawn by later authors, particularly those who lived in the early eighteenth century.

Unfortunately, historians of the twentieth century continue to identify with sixteenth and seventeenth century authors and accept as uncontested evidence some of their views on conditions in the Ottoman world. The opinions of writers as Koçu Bey constitute the source for the picture still found in quite a few twentieth century scholarly accounts of the Ottoman Empire. As a consequence, modern researchers who ought to know better still view Ottoman state and society not only as rigid and unchanging but also as intrinsically unchangeable. On one level, it might be said that twentieth century historians are victims of their sources, willing victims, to be sure, since the static image of Ottoman society as presented by the nasihatname authors lends itself admirably to political statements in a nineteenth and twentieth century context. From this perspective, it is certainly true that each generation writes its own history.

A significant example of what I would regard as misuse and misinterpretation of the nasihatname literature is the fact that assertions made by Mustafa 'Ali in the late sixteenth century or Koçu Bey in the seventeenth are taken, without further investigation, as proof for the decline of the Ottoman Empire.[35] Twentieth century scholars shy away from taking these tracts for what they are, partisan and political tracts that reflect a struggle within the ruling elite. I am suggesting that through analysis of the internal evidence found in these pieces and of the occasions for their production it is possible to demonstrate the exact opposite of rigidity, namely, a fluidity in the state and the societal norms. At the very least, closer scrutiny would reveal that what had been considered exceptional change in the earlier period had become prevalent by the end of the seventeenth century. To illustrate the change it is necessary not only to examine the picture projected by Ottoman contemporaries but also to reconstruct the historical reality of that particular era. At present, however, it seems that studies concerning Ottoman political writing of the sixteenth and seventeenth centuries are still carried on in virtual isolation from studies on contemporary Ottoman social and economic structure. Only when this artificial isolation has been overcome will a more critical evaluation of the nasihatnames become possible.

IV.

Nearly all the examples of the nasihatname genre examined here share one common feature: they teach *adab* (etiquette or "how to's"). For example, there are texts called *'adab al-ṣalatin*, which deal with how sultans should behave. Others are called *'adab al-kavanin*, an expression referring to the manner in which the *kanuns* or regulations should be read, understood, and applied. Thus, it would appear that the authors emphasize the practical orientation of their work; purportedly, the nasihatnames are intended primarily not as an exposition of historical fact or political philosophy, but as a guide to action. At the same time, it is possible that their authors were referring obliquely to the courtly adab literature of the Abbasid and later periods. After all, many writers of nasihatnames were themselves members of the Ottoman bureaucracy, and as such must have been familiar with the scribal culture of their medieval predecessors.

Two dimensions of the nasihat literature require clarification. First it should be noted that during certain periods the term prince was used generically, and could refer to anyone who shared in the power of coercion—although nearly always the literature appears to address the sultan who actually occupied the Ottoman throne at the time of its writing. Moreover, this literature was produced and reproduced even in circumstances when princes of the dynasty did not rule, but only reigned, as was the case with Ottoman sultans for most of the seventeenth century. In all probability, some of the advice literature produced in the seventeenth century was aimed at the ruling elite, to guide and advise them on how best to conduct themselves in the exercise of their power.

A second dimension of the nasihatname literature, and one that has caused a good deal of misunderstanding among modern researchers, is its self-proclaimed nature as advice literature. Most modern editors and translators of the texts have taken the claims they contain all too literally, and it is rare to find a modern commentator who will furnish the specific context in which a given nasihatname was produced. As a result, previous researchers have, for the most part, failed to see that many nasihatnames reflect the voice, the opinion, and the political point of view of one individual, or perhaps even more significantly, the position of certain elements from within the ruling class which had lost out in the struggle for power. In this sense, modern studies mislead the reader into thinking that the advice literature was a blueprint for guiding the policies of the current prince. When the literature is reproduced without taking into consideration the historical occasion for its composition, the reader is duped into believing that the

authors of the nasihatnames intended to formulate a structure for reform very much on the order of modern economic five-year plans. Rather than advice manuals or calls
for reform, the nasihatnames should be regarded mostly as
polemics, and only occasionally as protest pamphlets.

The approach I propose for the study of the nasihat literature was in part suggested by the critical observations
on Ottoman society and government written down by a
seventeenth century ʿalim from Egypt, al-Khafaji (d. ca.
1650; for a biography of Khafaji, see Appendix D). Khafaji
denounced the Ottoman elite in Istanbul with scathing,
unrestrained venom, which becomes understandable if his
personal fortunes are taken into account. Khafaji had come
to the Ottoman capital to make a career for himself, but
once there his good fortune was shortlived. By the time he
had settled down in Istanbul, he realized that limits had
been placed on the advancement and social mobility of
provincial elites. Therefore, he was unable to advance beyond the first stages of the high *ilmiye* career. Khafaji
failed to gain what he had hoped for or what he had felt
entitled to receive, and he ended up an exile in his home
province, filled with bitterness toward those officials
whom he associated with his personal frustration and dis-
appointment. It is highly probable that his uninhibited
accounts were meant as a protest rather than a well-
intentioned call for reform.

How are such examples interpreted in the scholarly literature? As has been indicated, most twentieth century
scholars take the nasihatname literature quite literally, as
descriptions of contemporary politics and society. Modern
researchers have accepted at face value the observations of
contemporary Ottoman writers. Some have taken the shift
in norms noted in the nasihatname as an indication of the
failure of the traditional societal system. Nor do twentieth
century scholars view the difficulties described by the
nasihatname writers as temporary setbacks. From their
perspective, the testimony of earlier authors is made to appear as a depiction of the steady, inevitable failure of an
entire social and political project. Scant attention is paid

to the uncomfortable fact that Ottoman state and society endured into the early part of the twentieth century. However it is necessary to explain the resilience of the system and its capacity for survival.

The writers of the nasihatnames claim historical authenticity for their descriptions and analyses. To document their faithful adherence to reality, they are careful to always use a specific date or reign as a watershed between the glorious past and the uncertain present. The dates most often selected fall in the closing years of the sixteenth century, for example, 996 A.H. (1588 C.E.), or 1000 (1591–92), or else the entire reign of Kanuni Süleyman is designated as such a watershed. Given the limited and strictly practical aims of most of the nasihatnames authors, it seems unreasonable to endow them with the omniscient capacity to reproduce the actual Ottoman social, political, and economic scene, whether of the remembered past or of their own time. It is safe to argue that at best, the pictures these authors draw are highly selective. A close reading of the sources reveals that in some cases the narratives turn out to be artificial constructs specifically and obviously colored by the authors' socioeconomic and political predelections. In other instances, the images border on outright fabrication, reflecting wishful thinking, vain hopes, or personal grievances. In other words, the nasihatnames can be regarded as ideological tracts designed to further specific political schemes, and sometimes aimed at the authors' return, whether as a class or as individuals, to a position of power and privilege. At other times, the tracts may have been written to show that certain people who held power at a given time were justified in the way they used it and that they should have retained their positions. Such seems to be the tone of the sixteenth century writer and former grand vezir, Lütfi Paşa, the author of the Asafname. He may not have wished to return to power, but even so, he blames outsiders for forcing him out of office.[36]

Reflecting on his own time, Mustafa 'Ali (1541–1600) regrets the decline of past standards, when what he calls merit, ability, and experience or wisdom formed the basis for appointments to prestigious and lucrative posts. He notes that some of his own contemporaries advanced in prestige, wealth, and careers not because of their merit and ability, but through influence, *intisap*. Intisap applies specifically to those who were part of the sultan's personal entourage or of the households of royal favorites. 'Ali thus equates change with corruption. In reality, he was caught in the midst of struggles that were due ultimately to the sociopolitical and economic changes within Ottoman society late in the sixteenth century. Even though a twentieth century reader may agree that 'Ali presents a picture of corruption in Ottoman society and that he hints at decline in Ottoman power (a view, incidentally, that is put forth more forcefully by Koçu Bey), one must be careful not to misinterpret his views as representing objective historical reality. 'Ali was not simply an observer, he was a disappointed participant in the events he decries; and in describing the changes in the world around him, he seems to be describing his own marginalization. He seems not to have understood why, try as he might, he was unable to break through and succeed in receiving the lucrative posts, honor, and prestige to which he felt his talents and experience entitled him. Recently, Cornell Fleischer has attempted to show exactly how, during the years 'Ali was trying to build his career, the expanding Ottoman bureaucracy was elaborating rules for recruitment and promotion.[37] These rules, however, turned out to be somewhat different from those which 'Ali, a product of the *medrese* (the religious school system) as it existed during Kanuni Süleyman's middle years, had come to expect. Now 'Ali was undoubtedly an experienced bureaucrat and an acute observer of his surroundings; even so, it is often difficult to perceive and evaluate overall patterns of change when they directly affect one's personal and political life. Moreover, even though 'Ali expressed his frustration and marginalization in characteristically personal terms, he was by no means unique in his plight. In fact, his outlook was shared by others who wrote "from the loser's point of view," for example, Koçu Bey and Khafaji.

All three authors—'Ali, Koçu Bey, and Khafaji—were dissatisfied with the existing order. 'Ali and Koçu Bey express their dissatisfaction by expressing their hopes for the return of princes with charismatic leadership, who would play an active and dynamic role from the center. Both authors criticize the dynasty for delegating authority to deputies (vukela) and boon companions (nudema), and both faulted royal associates for having become too powerful in their own right, and for using their position to advance members of their personal entourage to public posts in disregard of past protocol (kanuns, adab). Koçu Bey goes as far as expressing his unhappiness with change by calling for a return to a time when the feudal cavalry (the sipahis) was the dominant military force; the cavalry, he believed, would redress the balance of power, which had shifted in favor of the standing army (kapi kullari).

'Ali, like many others writing in the nasihatname genre, claims that he offered advice out of a sense of moral obligation to the ruler to tell the truth as he saw it. Thus he admonishes the sultan's well-wishers to become a "seeing eye for him" (wa yakunu lahu 'aynan nazirah) (7v), and states that "verily it is incumbent upon all to assist the sultan with advice" (fahaqun 'ala jami' alwara an yamudu als-sultan bilmunasahat) (7r).[38] By quoting the principles that impel individuals to counsel the sultans, 'Ali claims no personal stake in the matter. Yet at the beginning of his tract, he lists four pillars (i.e., chapters) that need to be upheld in order for justice and equity to prevail. The fourth pillar consists of a list of injuries and injustices which he felt had been unfairly heaped upon him personally. If the reader were to accept 'Ali's own formulation, then the reestablishment of equity and justice in the world becomes contingent upon his appointment to high office. (In a personal communication, Cornell Fleischer disagrees with this interpretation; he thinks 'Ali meant to say that he was not afraid of telling the truth, not that he had nothing at stake. Nevertheless, Fleischer's alternative interpretation does not consider the significance of 'Ali's using his own misfortunes to illustrate the disruption of the world order.)

V.

When expressed in a systematic fashion, Koçu Bey's ideal image of state and society, as far as can be discerned through his ideological and political filters, has the following features (some of which 'Ali shares):

> The sultan is a scion of the Ottoman dynasty and is at the top of the ladder. He possesses charisma, a main hallmark of his leadership, and runs public affairs from the center and in person without delegating authority to anyone. (Appendix B below provides a detailed outline of the major issues raised by Koçu Bey's *Risale.*)

Public service is founded on merit. Appointments are also based on a standard of public service that is predicated on experience. Dismissal without cause is not tolerated. The duration of most appointments extends from a long tenure to life, the argument being that the effective functioning of officers in most orders of society is guaranteed by a long-term appointment with an implied hereditary passage of office. The early modern merit system espoused here is a closed one, which applies only to a particular sector of society. In theory, the system tolerates only the most minimal social mobility.

Incumbent grand vezirs should be free from any outside interference, even from the royal court. The grand vezir must have direct access to the sultan, and what passes between them must remain secret. It may not be shared with anyone, not even with other vezirs. The sipahi or cavalry order serves as the right hand of the sultans, who are sustained by a feudal system. Those assigned as sipahis are given *ziamets* and timars (fiefs) for such extended periods of time that their appointments become virtually hereditary. It is expected that feudal appointments will be passed from father to son or to next of kin. Such a structure might be adequately described as hereditary, military, and feudal.

Koçu Bey defines the *kul* order (standing army, including the janissaries), spells out the rules for recruitment into the corps, indicates what *ulufe* (salaries) are paid to corps members, and duly notes the sources of these salaries. Unlike the sipahi order, the *kullar* remain limited and circumscribed in their political role and are relegated to purely instrumental functions. Koçu Bey contends that the loyalty of the sipahis, if they are satisfied with long-term appointments, is demonstrated by their ability to control the kul. Assured of their future, the sipahis can be expected again to form the vanguard in battles for the expansion of the realms of Islam. Since they come from the ranks of the people (reaya), the sipahis are not likely to act contrary to the interests of the taxpaying subjects. Koçu Bey clearly states that the sipahis were originally reaya, which means that at some unspecified time in the past, a transition from taxpayer to military man and official was in fact possible. Koçu Bey does not imply that he is in favor of mobility for the reaya; rather, he simply contrasts the sipahi with the kul, who in his view are far more remote from the concerns of the peasanty and therefore more inclined to place intolerable burdens upon the taxpayers.

The learned *ulema* constitute an order which is treated very much like that of the sipahis; appointments to ulema positions are also virtually for life. Hereditary right to office is assured, although it is predicated on the successful completion of a *cursus honorum*. At the same time, merit and service are important criteria for appointment and promotion. The combination of hereditary rights and insistence on merit and experience gives the established ruling class a monopoly over public service.

These three orders—the sipahi, kul and ulema—make up the society, meaning here those permitted to participate in political affairs. Members of each order know their place and adhere to the *rasm* (rules or prescriptions) and adab (etiquette or constitution) of their respective orders. There is a prohibition against crossing class lines.

Koçu Bey assumes that men in public service are motivated principally by ethical and pious considerations. It is these inner qualities possessed by statesmen and public servants that propel them forward and guide them in the performance of their public responsibilities. On closer examination of Koçu Bey's model, it becomes clear that not too far behind ethical and pious considerations lies the self-interest of established members of the Ottoman political class: Tenure is of long duration, and in practically all the orders (with the principal exception of the standing army of kullar) the possessions that accompany appointment, if not the office itself, are hereditary. One is dismissed from office only for flagrant infractions of the norm. Although dismissal for "just cause" leads to loss of position, Koçu Bey still recommends that the sons of the deposed should inherit position and material support, for it is the perpetuation of hereditary advantages that ensures loyalty.

The various parts of the social structure constitute a centralized system of governance. The sultan stands at the head of a pyramid of hierarchies composed of aristocracies which monopolize their prescribed place in society, politics, and the economy. An appointee within the system performs his official duties spontaneously, as if by natural impulse. His motives are ethical and moral. Only those who have experience are appointed to positions of public service, after they have passed through the ranks and the prescribed career paths. Underlying these prescriptions is the assumption that all members of the Ottoman state administration partake of a common "high" culture, considered to be the path of merit. High culture may be acquired in different places in accordance with the order to which a given individual belongs. For ulema, the center for obtaining high culture will be the medrese. For all others, the literary salons (*maclis*) in the houses of influential bureaucrats and the lodges of *dervishes* function in a similar manner. But most particularly, the special institution for acquiring high culture is the sultan's palace. Irrespective of where this culture is first acquired, however, what counts is the fact that it has been acquired, and its acquisition constitutes entry into the path of merit. This is perhaps how one should interpret Koçu Bey's insistence that entry into the Ottoman political class should be allowed only to those outsiders or foreigners who have spent time in the service of a foreign king, for presumably their acquisition of high culture makes up for the defect of being outsiders.

Each order is basically self-governing and is to be given autonomy of action. For example, punishing members of their own order for infractions of their own regulations (kanuns or etiquette) is incumbent upon the higher-ranking dignitaries of each order. Candidates for vacancies are selected internally, with no interference from the palace or even the sultan, who should not countermand what the grand vezir has decreed.

When looked at through Koçu Bey's eyes, this world does indeed represent the realization of an early modern bureaucrat's dream: everything in its prescribed place, with its rules and regulations, and once adopted, a system functioning to perfection and without unforeseen complications. It is a centralized system, where rewards and promotions are based on estate-bound or class-bound merit and service rather than on informal influence. As long as social, economic, and career lines are maintained (and those who are raised in a particular line do not cross over into another type of career), all is well, and the world order or nizam-i alem is preserved. (The image of state and society Koçu Bey formulates has features in common with the picture that medieval and early modern European authors have reconstructed of the estate system in their period of study.)[39]

When boon companions become imperial advisors on public affairs of the state (devlet-i aliyye) and when the peasants (reaya) make pretensions at being members of the military order trouble starts and the balance of the Ottoman early modern system breaks down. The proper order of the world is predicated upon all knowing their place and

function and remaining in it, exhibiting no further ambi-
tion or aspiration for social mobility. In fact, more than
minimal social mobility is not tolerated. Such is the picture that emerges from Koçu Bey's account of the ideal
functioning of the Ottoman political class.

While all the nasihatnames contain lengthy discussions and descriptions of the orders that make up the ruling class, they are consistently brief in their treatment of
the peasants (reaya), whose portrayal is purely negative.
All the authors agree that the reaya have to be confined
within their traditional bounds and watched carefully, lest
they mistake official laxity in the enforcement of social
distinctions and regulations for weakness. Laxity towards
the kanun can lead to the reaya's infringing upon the privileges of the other orders, and they may consider themselves as actually belonging to another (higher) order and
act accordingly. The infringement of the reaya upon the
domain of the *askeri* is to be taken as one reason for the
existing social, political, and economic chaos. Thus vigi-
lance in the management and control of the reaya is a
standard admonition in almost all of the nasihatnames.

It should be noted that all the nasihatname writers
belong to the ruling class, hence their emphasis on the rulers, who as far as they are concerned, are the most important elements in society. The authors devote far more
space to the delineation of the duties, responsibilities, and
etiquette of the ruling class than to those of the reaya.

In at least one tract, Koçu Bey's *Risale*, the author's
social ideals are presented as a replication of a state and
society that once existed. But despite the recurrent insistence by both Koçu Bey and 'Ali on the historicity of their
model—a model characterized by a highly centralized authority dominating a virtually immobile society—they actually projected their own idealized fantasies onto the past.
The situations they describe never existed. It is highly im-
probable that at any point in Ottoman history sultans had
the absolute monopoly of power that these accounts at-
tribute to them. The nasihatname writers would have
readers believe that the sultans exercised power without

regard to the ruling elites who were allied to them in the exploitation of the material resources of the Empire. Quite apart from the fact that few known societies have ever functioned in this manner, the sultan and the ruling elite both derived so many advantages from their alliance that the ideological distortion in the nasihatname accounts is immediately apparent.

The picture Koçu Bey draws is one of a powerful sultan commanding and exercising complete control over a centrally managed society. Yet at the same time, the sipahis and the ulema constitute virtual aristocracies. Following their own protocol or rasm and governed by their own constitution or kanun, the orders are all but autonomous, appointing candidates to offices and dismissing officials when necessary. Koçu Bey's assertions of and hopes for a presumed harmony and balance to the contrary, social conflict between the ruling class and the peasants and the political struggle among members of the ruling class were inevitable. But in the late fifteenth century and the first half of the sixteenth, conflicts were held at a minimum, since a consensus operated among the ruling elite. The dynasty and the different levels the aristocracy had reached a basic agreement on how to manage the Empire, and therefore the ruling class was able to muster enough force to impose its will on the rest of society. Even with respect to the early and middle sixteenth century, however, Koçu Bey is making a statement of doubtful validity. In the fourteenth and fifteenth centuries, when the Ottoman Empire was expanding on its western front, considerable tension existed among the ruling group. After Mehmed the Conqueror (1451–1481), had reconstituted the Ottoman governing class, members of the old elites who had not managed to enter the charmed circle protested and his successor Bayezid II had to accommodate them. In the reign of Süleyman the Lawgiver (1520–1566) struggles between his sons engaged considerable sections of the ruling class, and the sixteenth century was punctuated by tribal rebellions, occasionally under the leadership of pre-Ottoman princely families of Anatolia.

VI.

Throughout Koçu Bey's treatise, he reiterates the need
to give the officers independence for the duration of their
tenure. Writers such as Koçu Bey and 'Ali claim to view
office as a fixed entity with defined functions, procedures,
and rules, hence the emphasis on the adab dimension of
the discussion. It is quite inconceivable to them that an
office can be turned into an investment whose purpose is
profit pure and simple. At least, this is how they claim to
perceive the problem. It can be argued also, however, that
office was treated as income not only in the time of Koçu
Bey in the seventeenth century, but also in the later
sixteenth-century when 'Ali was writing. Moreover, the
same applied to the so-called classical period, as evidenced
by early sixteenth century liva kanunnameleri: here the
monetary penalties for infringements of the kanun (or *cer-
ayim*) are treated as income that devolves on the governor
of a district, or on the sipahi in whose timar the violation
has taken place. The office of the *muhtesip* (the inspector
of market prices, measures, and weights) in the early sixteenth century also constitutes an excellent example of
how the office might be treated mainly as a source of income. In other words, the nasihatname authors' renditions
of the classical period are mere projections of an idealized
picture onto the past.

VII.

When Koçu Bey in his *Risale* describes the state and
society of his time, he begins by addressing, under the
heading "Status of the Sultans and Vezirs," two issues he
regards as crucial: the delegation of authority, and the
blurring of distinctions and demarcations between social
orders. He faults the sultans for withdrawing from the conduct of public affairs and for delegating their authority.
Worse yet, royal companions and palace favorites have

taken over government functions by monopolizing access to the sultans, thereby circumventing the grand vezir's authority. Koçu Bey gives the year 982 (1574–75) as the critical date when the vezirs lost their freedom of action and when palace favorites began to dominate politics. From then onwards, vezirs were appointed by the members of inner court cliques, and as a result grand vezirs were able to stay in office for only comparatively short periods of time.

Koçu Bey, like 'Ali before him, expresses his concern over the blurring of distinctions between the social orders that made up the Ottoman political class. The dissolution of differentiation was especially evident when the personal entourage of the vezirs, paşas, and court favorites were assigned living allowances (*dirliks*) from the public treasury. Whole villages and farms were turned from assignments that benefited the soldiery into sources of revenue for courtiers (especially in the form of the *paşmakliks* or fiefs as a form of "shoe money" for royal princesses, and *arpaliks*, "fiefs of barley," for the grandees).

To the nasihatname writers, the most significant dimension of awarding office as income to palace favorites and others was the fact that the practice downgraded the military dimension of the office. Those who had taken over zeamets and timars ceased to live up to the military obligations of their offices. Office-seeking had turned into a competition for lucrative sources of gain, although offices were not necessarily assigned a specific income. Even when an assignment was made, the income might well be insufficient for the increasing expenses of many public officials. Each officeholder had to be constantly on the lookout for additional sources of income, often acquiring them by a method which amounted to a purchase at auction, a process over which there was little control. For those who lacked the resources to bid for extra sources of income, the system of appointments had become a fraud, an impious act based on greed. Those on the inside, however, did what they believed they were entitled to do, without regard for the admonitions of Koçu Bey, 'Ali, and others like them.

In the late sixteenth and in the seventeenth centuries social distinctions were becoming less rigid, an indication of social mobility. For Koçu Bey and 'Ali, the increased mobility of the Ottoman ruling class was reflected in negligence in maintaining the external signs and symbols that distinguished one order from another, such as the sumptuary laws. Men of all classes were seen riding horses and donning swords, activities that once were the privilege of the higher orders. Koçu Bey even attributed the social protests of provincial soldiers, known as the Celali rebellions, to infringements of the kanun. It is clear that Koçu Bey himself observed symptoms of dissolution in the social distinctions that had been known in the past.

What follows is a summary of the trends that Koçu Bey's *Risale* presents as contemporary changes in the state and societal system of his time.

1. A breakdown was taking place in whatever consensus had existed earlier among the ruling elite with respect to the sharing of benefits and responsibilities. As evidence, Koçu Bey adduces the fierce competition for place and appointment which characterized a system that had become more open-ended than it had been in the past. Upward mobility and loss of social status were also more prevalent. In the earlier arrangement of state and society, as sketched by Koçu Bey, an appointment to office and one's place in society were prescribed by heredity and an in-class merit system on the one hand, and long tenure in office on the other. In Koçu Bey's own time, office—be it as a sipahi, janissary, or administrator—was available for pay and assigned to the highest bidder, or else acquired through influence. Officeholding had lost its former association with function and was now perceived as open to wealthy individuals regardless of class affiliation. Appointments were now made for limited periods of time, suggesting a scarcity of revenues, and incumbents were expected to step aside for others who were waiting their turn.

2. The power and position of the sultan had become marginal and symbolic. The ruler was isolated from the daily routines of public service and power. That Koçu Bey and 'Ali correctly observed this change is borne out by subsequent historical developments. Sometime after the publication of their tracts, the type of sultan that both Koçu Bey and 'Ali had hoped to see did in fact ascend the throne, but he was unable to maintain his position for long. Apparently those sultans who could not adapt to a more circumscribed role were deposed, and in their place more conciliatory rulers were appointed (in the first half of the seventeenth century, Murad IV's seemingly independent stance is a rare exception).[40] Marginalized as masters (or even partners) of the ruling elite, the sultans were able to retain their positions only as long as they were willing to play the mostly symbolic role assigned to them. In fact, the elevating or deposing of sultans signaled a contest between competing factions within the ruling elite.

3. The social system of orders had broken down: anyone could enter any order. This obtained not only for the military but also for the ilmiye and the ruling elite. The change was particularly apparent within the ilmiye. For most of the seventeenth century and even the very early part of the eighteenth, nearly half of the new recruits for the Istanbul high ilmiye came from merchant or artisan backgrounds. The new recruits came to equal in number those drawn from high ilmiye families, that is, the aristocratic families that had brought forth high-level ulema for at least three generations.[41] Members of the reaya order also were no longer confined to their prescribed place in the economy or the society. Peasants abandoned their assigned plots, moved into the cities, and become artisans. Those who failed to find a niche for themselves resorted to rebellion and brigandage, a form of resistance to their changed socioeconomic position. This state of flux was in direct contrast to the equilibrium that had characterized the classical period, and was perceived by the nasihatname writers as a dra-

matic change. After all, the only mobility that Koçu Bey was willing to concede involved the exceptional individuals who entered Ottoman state employment after having served other rulers, in most cases at the court of Iran.

4. The system of surplus extraction was undergoing major change. There was an ongoing battle for maximizing immediately realizable revenues. In this respect, the observations of the nasihatname writers are quite accurate; a study of the Ottoman taxation system in the later sixteenth and seventeenth centuries does, in fact, show that irregular taxes such as *avariz* and *sürsat* carried more weight than the *oşür* and other taxes registered in the liva kanunnamleri. According to the registers of important affairs (*mühimme defterleri*), Ottoman taxpayers, recognizing the "novelty" of these taxes, frequently resisted the unprecedented demands for revenue.[42]

5. Another emerging characteristic of the Ottoman state that caught the imagination of the nasihatname authors was the sale of office. They bewail the conversion of appointments to public office into a money-making and money-raising proposition and the incumbents' neglect of their duties of office, and conclude that the primary goal of each appointee during his short tenure in office was to maximize the return on his investment.

6. Fiscal regulations such as the liva kanunnameleri or social and political rules such as the kanun or rasm, which had once governed the orders making up Ottoman state and society had become largely irrelevant. The manner in which the writers of the nasihatnames treat the rules and regulations is most revealing of their political views. Most importantly, they perceive the regulations as givens, and tolerate no change. One might almost say that they view state and society not only as rigid and unchanging but also as unchangeable. Particularly, they give primacy to legal rulings over the practical real life occasions those rulings had originally been meant to suit. For example, many provincial *kanunnames* state that reaya who left their villages without

the permission of the timar-holder could be forced to return within a stipulated time period, which varied between ten and twenty years. This regulation made sense in times of labor scarcity. After 1550, however, and before the Celali rebellions of the 1550s and early 1600s led to flight from the villages and population contraction, labor was not scarce, which may explain why the old regulation was allowed to lapse.[43] Authors like 'Ali or Koçu Bey did not even hint at such changes in the balance of Ottoman society, and it is only when nineteenth and twentieth century scholars gained access to archival documents that the one-sided views of the nasihatname authors became clearly apparent.

7. While most of the tracts contain lengthy discussions and descriptions of all the orders which composed the Ottoman ruling class, they are consistently brief in their treatment of the common people (reaya). Given their implied assumption that the whole social system would collapse without proper control of the reaya, the nasihatname authors consistently advocated constant watch over the sultan's subjects.

8. The accounts of society and the state given in the nasihatnames reflect the end of the early modern form of centralization that prevailed in the classical period and of its accompanying corollary, the class-bound merit system that had once regulated public service and societal divisions. It may be recalled that these features were characteristic of the Ottoman system at a time when there was a consensus among the ruling elite concerning the division of services and taxes extracted from Ottoman taxpayers. The new experimentation in revenue extraction signaled a change in the system as a whole.

VIII.

'Ali and Koçu Bey looked back to what they thought had prevailed in the recent past, namely, an early modern centralization, a corresponding early modern merit system, and charismatic leadership by the sultans. But during the time in which they lived and wrote, the old order was gradually disintegrating. In the second half of the seventeenth century, the dissolution of the old order led ultimately to a consolidation of power by an essentially civilian oligarchy composed of neither the sipahi order nor the standing army. Whereas 'Ali and Koçu Bey had advocated the return to a time when an aristocratic sipahi order was in control, the literary champion of the new civilian oligarchy was Mustafa Naima.[44]

A close scrutiny of the dedicatory preface in Naima's *History* and the relevant section on state and society reveals an underlying meaning not stated in so many words, a frequent occurrence in Ottoman historical literature. Like other Ottoman historians, Naima relies on traditional sources and precedents, such as the *Muqadima* of Ibn Khaldun and *Akhlaq-'Ala'i*, among others.[45] The pattern of reliance on intellectual predecessors should alert us to a consistent tendency among the authors of historical literature to demonstrate that their arguments have precedents, and therefore are not new. Their intention was to show contemporary Ottoman readers that the sociopolitical formation developing right before their eyes in the late seventeenth century was not unnatural, but rather, the result of legitimate change within the framework of a well-established tradition.

Naima devotes little space to the discussion of the state (devlet). Instead, he focuses first on the nature of society and the definition and composition of its orders or classes, and then on the acceptable ranges of change the society allows. Naima takes his discussion of change through a fairly elaborate discourse on transitional periods. It should be noted that the term change should be understood as "legitimate change," or "limits of change," or "limited and gradual change" to distinguish it from the type of violent change usually associated with social revolution. Naima keeps his discussion at a theoretical level, and the examples he uses are invariably taken from historically distant periods. The choice is deliberate. The author adopts this form of expression in order to show that change in society had taken place in every period of history, and that the emergence of new orders or classes was not an unprecedented occurrence. By resorting to the most ancient examples and avoiding direct reference to more recent or contemporary events, Naima may have intended to persuade his readers that change is for the most part a product of historical or impersonal forces, and therefore inevitable. What is left out of the equation is social or human action. Naima equally avoids reference to the social or class struggles prevalent at the time. His insistence on natural-historical precedents for change may well have been aimed, at least in part, at discouraging active resistance by those excluded from the elite who might otherwise have felt the need to ameliorate their socioeconomic or political condition. Naima's judgment may be regarded as a conservative argument in defense of change. At the same time, he and his predecessors gloss over the social, and therefore the human, dimension involved.

In this context, it is instructive to study how seventeenth century Ottoman sources treated the removal of sultans from the throne. For example, among the listed causes for Sultan Ibrahim's deposition (1058/1648) we find eschatological and natural phenomena, including ill omens, which are said to have coincided with the day of the unfortunate sultan's birth.[46] The chronicles report that earthquakes and plagues marked the inauspicious occasion and boded ill for Ibrahim's subsequent reign. The implication is, of course, that no human being need be considered responsible for Ibrahim's deposition, which then becomes purely a matter of fate.

Also aimed at eliminating the human dimension of change is another device closely associated with the supernatural one: an organic view of society. Here society is made to follow a natural or biological course of birth, maturity, and decline or death. For example, the participants in the 1703 rebellion protested that their goal was not political struggle and social strife, which they claimed would result in chaos. Instead, they wanted to restore order to the world. Thus again the refrain is repeated: change cannot be seen as a product of struggle, and therefore it is not the result of human or social action. Some sources on the 1703 rebellion implicitly deny the role of legitimate human action in change by portraying dissident soldiers as acting out of pure selfishness, seeking immediate enjoyment of the fruits of their struggle. Contemporary chroniclers condemn as unbecoming and crude this wish for immediate gratification. The resort to pseudo-biological, supernatural, and selfish motives in the narrative itself seems to conceal a desire for legitimating what was actually in process. On the whole, the narrative sources concerning the 1703 rebellion convey an image of change not too far removed from Naima's account. They seem anxious to portray change in a legitimizing light, emphasizing its moderation as they deny it a social dynamic. In contrast to Naima's highly structured and abstract view of social change, the historical reality of the times was replete with turmoil and struggle, conflict, and resistance. Social change was manifested in the dissolution of old practices and the slow but systematic consolidation of new ones.[47]

It should be recalled that Naima's treatise was completed at the turn of the eighteenth century. These years constitute a critical juncture in the process of socioeconomic and sociopolitical change in Ottoman society. The process had been going on for a long time, observed not only by Koçu Bey in the first half of the seventeenth century and 'Ali in the late sixteenth, but even earlier by Lütfi Paşa during the reign of Kanuni Süleyman (1520–1566).[48] Around 1700, however, when a sultan had just been deposed (for consenting to a disastrous peace treaty), and provincial notables had many parts of the Ottoman realm under firm control, the process of political change was more dramatically visible than at any time previously.

One dimension of the political change is manifested by the transformation that was taking place in the composition of the ruling elite in Istanbul and in the provinces in the second half of the seventeenth century.[49] For the purposes of this study, it is useful to reconstruct this statistically verifiable political change partly because it constitutes the historical context for later transformations. An analysis of the phenomenon will permit us to offer a set of guiding interpretations that may inform a future research program for the study of Ottoman state and society in the seventeenth century.

By the second half of the seventeenth century and the beginning of the eighteenth, there was open acceptance of the receding power of the palace, of the sipahi order, and of the janissaries. The palace's waning influence is exemplified in the latter part of the seventeenth century by the very process of selection for succession to the Ottoman throne. In the second half of the century, three sultans were appointed and two removed by sociopolitical forces not connected to the dynastic family or palace circles.[50] Furthermore, the forces that now were making and unmaking sultans did not belong to any social groups which traditionally (and therefore normally) had been associated with such activities in the past, such as, the sipahi or, more usually, the military (askeri) order. Since the dynasty had lost much of its former power, the charismatic model of leadership also became irrelevant. In its place, a collective leadership, based in a civilian oligarchy became consolidated. By the second half of the seventeenth century, most of the sultans acted mainly as symbolic leaders, providing a facade of continuity for the old practices as they helped to legitimate new ones. This phenomenon was in direct contrast to developments in contemporary Western Europe, where absolute monarchies, justified by the ideology of divine right were consolidating their powers and sanctioning royal usurpation of political and economic initiatives from the traditional landed aristocracy. The divergent course of the Ottoman historical experience may be illustrated by the fact that the era of Ottoman grandees was only just beginning, whereas European grandees were losing their power to centralizing monarchies, often after a series of external or civil wars.

In the Ottoman case, a substantial and successful change occurred in the recruitment and the material underpinnings of the ruling class. It may be recalled that both 'Ali and Koçu Bey had provided description and analysis of this change.[51] In a way, Naima picks up the story where 'Ali and Koçu Bey leave off, and it is useful to compare Naima's account with our own reconstruction of the same historical phenomenon.

The introduction of new elements into the Ottoman ruling class has been noted in earlier publications.[52] Although the older members of the Ottoman elite continued to exercise a certain degree of power together with the new members, a struggle ensued between the two groups which ultimately netted the newcomers the lion's share of the most important and lucrative appointments in and of the Empire. Naima acted as a spokesman for the "new" constituents of the ruling elite. The changes which he qualifies in his introduction as precedented, normal, and perhaps even classical, are the very ones that actually describe the rise to prominence of the new group.

In his treatise Naima lumps together under the rubric "military" a variety of old factions of the ruling class. According to his vision, the military could be expected to thrive in a period of military expansion. Upholding the biological analogy of birth, maturation, decline, and death, for historical development, Naima contends that by the end of the seventeenth century the Ottoman state had reached the middle of its life span, which was the period for civilians to run the state and be its chief beneficiaries. In a period of tranquility and consolidation, he explains, military skills are not needed as much as administrative capabilities. The takeover by the civilian faction to whose ascendance Naima alludes was completed by the end of the seventeenth century, so that during the last two decades forty households controlled more than half of the appointments to high office. Moreover, the heads of these households tried to perpetuate their influence by providing recruits for public service from their own personal households. In the process, they edged out both the palace factions and the military from most of the highest public posts. A new style of governance, which might be called "grandee politics," had come to prevail. In combination with factions from the high ilmiye order, beneficiaries of the new political system managed to make and unmake sultans, installing princes of their choice in the office of sultan, and depose those who were unwilling to cooperate.

The new power of the grandees was made possible by a series of changes in the material underpinnings of the new sections of the ruling class, which benefited the new elements more than anyone else. One of the most significant sources of income for the heads of the grandee households of the time was the pious foundation or *waqf/vakif.*

Most references to vakif by Ottoman writers of the sixteenth or early seventeenth century, and in the twentieth century scholarly literature, concentrate on the legal loopholes that were used to convert public lands into semi-private property through religious or pious foundations. It should be kept in mind that alienating public lands and property to the vakif benefited not only the families of the founders and endowed persons but also the ulema, who served as the guardians (*nazirs*) of these endowments. The founder's family retained some measure of control over the benefits that accrued from this wealth while at the same time, acquiring permanent provisions for its own upkeep. Succeeding generations could benefit from an independent and relatively secure base for the perpetuation of material wealth, immune from confiscations.

Through the *nezarets* (guardianships) of innumerable endowments, the ulema, especially the high ulema, developed a formidable financial and political power, which they wielded through the administration of endowment revenues. In addition, the ulema controlled the interpretation of articles and terms in the foundation deeds, or *vakfiyes.* The management of a wealth unparalleled in earlier periods also made the ilmiye career attractive. In fact, the ulema career became the career of choice for an individual seeking the highest material and monetary rewards, with a comparatively lower risk to life, limb, or property than in military or scribal careers. Throughout Ottoman history, with few exceptions, members of the ilmiye were immune from persecution and prosecution. Part of their special status derived from the fact that they served as guardians of the din, religion. Ottoman Islam was the ideology through which the ulema order gained nearly total immunity. Even though religion was at the heart of the ideology, however, the continued support and favor offered the ulema in the political and social arenas throughout the Empire's history require thorough and systematic study. Remarkably enough, this historiographical issue must be counted among the least studied in Ottoman scholarship.

Along with the conversion of private and individual wealth into endowments, there were more direct and officially sanctioned methods of alienating public lands. Sultanic decree could make feudal holdings such as ziamets and timars into crown lands often assigned to palace favorites.[53] It may be recalled that in an earlier period, namely, the second half of the sixteenth century, 'Ali had observed conversions of this type that were carried out contrary to the practice and rules that governed and protected the income of the sipahi order. Koçu Bey noted the same violations in the first half of the seventeenth century. It is to conversions of timars into crown lands and revenue assignments to palace favorites that both authors had attributed the virtual disappearance of the sipahi order.

Public (miri) lands were occasionally transformed into inheritable private property (mülk) by sultanic fiat. Some official documents implementing the surrender of public land contain interesting references to the status of the peasants who had lived on what were once miri lands. Certain documents granting freehold possession not only draw boundaries and limits for the alienated lands, they also register the peasants on those lands and thereby connect them to the private property in question. In other words, once the land had become private property, free peasants lost their freedom.[54] If this practice was indeed widespread in the later seventeenth century, as I am proposing here, it should have had far-reaching implications. The growth of private land ownership and the resulting peasant dependence are matters still hotly debated among

specialists. The most recent contributions tend to mini-
mize the incidence of this phenomenon. Even if this view
remains the consensus of future scholars, the appearance
of newly dependent peasants should tell us something
about the nature of the social formation which emerged by
the second half of the seventeenth century.[55]

It is my contention in this study that the seventeenth
century was a period of major upheavals, characterized
partially by external pressures and in the main by internal
social, economic, and political change. One example is the
transfer of public lands into private property. If future research bears me out, then one focal point of study should
be the rise of a new social formation commensurate with
newly identified economic realities, that must take account of the accumulation of wealth by new social sectors
of society. At the same time, the various forms of resistance to the developing social formation must also catch
the attention of researchers.

When attention is drawn to the rarely studied practice
of *müsadere* (confiscation), another element providing a
material base for the new class becomes apparent.[56] The
secondary literature describes the royal confiscation of officials' property as a tool that permitted the sultans to
clear potential political obstacles to the dynasty's direct
rule over Ottoman public affairs. There were specific
historical circumstances to explain a growing, noticeable,
and obviously conscious but *selective* enforcement of the
müsadere prerogative, late in the seventeenth century.
Twentieth century researchers, however, take an ahistorical approach to the müsadere practice in claiming that it
was retained unchanged over time. The false impression is
therefore upheld that throughout the early modern period,
the sultans continued to enjoy an unchallenged political
status by exercising the power to deprive a contending social class of its power (material) base through the enforcement of müsadere. Yet, the enforcement of müsadere
varied over time and became especially dramatic in the
second half of the eighteenth century. At the same time,
Ottomans who should have been immune because of their

noninvolvement in government business, were liable to have their properties confiscated. In the scholarly literature the sultan's postulated ability to confiscate has been used to explain why a propertied, landed elite with an independent material base did not challenge the prerogatives of the sultans. Since the müsadere supposedly remained intact as an instrument for the dynasty's unchallenged reign and rule, it is possible to assume that even as late as the seventeenth century, public lands and property were regarded as something that the state could not permanently alienate. The continuing application of müsadere right into the nineteenth century has been taken by scholars as testimony of the tenacity of the view that Ottoman society had no land-based aristocracy.[57]

A marked change in the exercise of the müsadere prerogative can be discerned by the second half of the seventeenth century, when confiscation of the properties of deposed, disgraced, or deceased public servants became less frequent. A cursory review of the contemporary chronicles and archival records furnishes ample evidence for this change. Although the texts claim that confiscations are still the order of the day, very few assets of disgraced or deceased officials are singled out for expropriation. An even more significant aspect of the müsadere policy is the question of who could initiate or prevent confiscations. From the available evidence, it appears that the option was exercised at the discretion of whichever faction among the ruling class had the upper hand at the time. This was especially true when new factions had just succeeded to a position of power and when a victorious faction exercised the right of müsadere against those who had lost out.[58] The corollary to the rise of a new political elite with its peculiar bases of wealth and power, was a growing instability within the Ottoman ruling establishment.

Evidence from the late seventeenth century indicates a loosening of the barriers between the various social orders or classes (*tabakat*) of official Ottoman society, which, if one were to take the officially stated view, should have been rigid and permanent. The social and political fluidity was accompanied by strong indications of a breakdown in ethical and moral standards of daily life, or to use a different formulation, a breakdown in the binding powers of the dominant ideology. The sources refer to this breakdown in euphemistic terms as a laxity in adhering to the tenets of the din, religion. More significantly, the resulting historical phenomena are portrayed as "acts of evil-doing" and "lack of discipline," suggestive of individuals or groups acting on their own initiative, perhaps with an inclination to rebel. A few examples will be cited in illustration.

The first instance looks innocuous enough on the surface, but in fact hits at the core of Ottoman social stratification because it questions the definition of sociopolitical functions, statuses, and roles of groups and classes. At a critical point in the campaigns of the later seventeenth century, when the Ottoman Empire was hard-pressed for manpower, a group of military men invited the ulema to abandon the protective shield of their class and participate in campaigns as active combatants.[59] Some members of the ilmiye responded by enunciating a major principle in the "constitution" of Ottoman society, indeed of Islamic society in general. They read out to the military challengers that society is composed of four orders (tabakat), each with a clearly defined function: the military has the function to do battle; members of the ilmiye are responsible for the moral good of the community; merchants and peasants also have their assigned roles. These definitions and functions are viewed as eternal.[60] In a crisis, however, the barriers between the social orders or tabakat may break down. To cite one obvious example, all classes are expected to participate in the mobilization for Holy War, the cihad. Thus the corporate division into functions should be taken as a general rule, but one that has its exceptions. Prominent members of the ilmiye, such as Şeyhülislam Feyzullah Efendi, did in fact occasionally adopt the role of military commander.[61]

Another phenomenon observed by contemporaries points to the disappearance of the external signs that differentiated various social groups in Ottoman society. During the second half of the seventeenth century, frequent official decrees reaffirmed the behavior and dress codes for members of the Ottoman administration and for the subject population. Included were such stipulations as who was to ride a horse or carry a sword, and color codes for clothing to be worn by different members of the Ottoman population. To explain the insistence upon dress codes, the texts affirm that violations of the dress codes not only make it difficult to differentiate between classes, but also between women and men and between members of different *millets*.[62] The disregard for dress codes was hardly a new phenomenon, however. As indicated previously, similar behavior had already been noted by 'Ali and Koçu Bey in their respective periods.

It should be noted that by the second half of the seventeenth century, members of the military no longer acted as a monolithic unit and as a class, but rather like any other sector of society in which a variety of interests was represented. Thus, military men reacted in terms of their immediate interest as individuals or factions within the larger context of their corporate class.[63]

A last example is drawn from an unusual set of decrees issued to rectify widespread acts described only euphemistically, and whose redress was alluded to by the expression "proper faith is good advice" (ad-din ul-nasiha).[64] (For translation of texts see Appendix C). From the official point of view, laxity in adherence to the tenets of the faith was tantamount to immoral acts (mekruh). But apparently, the decrees meant to condemn something much more specific, namely, indulgence in magical acts and superstitious or pagan practices. The underlying meaning of the decrees, however, is inferred from the historical context. The decrees were issued as rebellions were breaking out in the Balkan and Crimean provinces. The latter were triggered by the economic hardships and social dislocations in Ottoman frontier society due to the territorial compromises laid down in the treaties of Karlowitz (1699) and Istanbul (1703). In the eyes of the state, however, resistance to the concessions and territorial losses was portrayed in the decrees as failure in proper indoctrination and acculturation. Therefore the admonition, ad-din ul-nasiha, which literally translates as "proper faith is in being properly guided (by accepting advice)," is therefore meant to enjoin absolute obedience by subjects to those in authority. Since the taking of advice is equated with an education in Islamic culture and ethos, officially the decrees are perceived as a serious breakdown in the binding powers of the ideology. Consistent with this analysis then, the decrees portray this breakdown as a grave deficiency on the part of the ulema, the remedy sought for meeting the social unrest is therefore found in the assignment of fresh, learned, and zealous recruits as teachers and preachers.[65]

IX.

The observations on state and society and the analyses outlined above concern the historical developments Ottoman society experienced in the latter half of the seventeenth century. Until further research is carried out, the following tentative generalizations are offered as a guide to interpretations and future research on Ottoman state and society in the early modern period.

First of all, it is necessary to reaffirm a simple truism which has been consistently denied in the scholarly literature: Ottoman society, like all human societies throughout history, was fluid and dynamic. Moreover, it retained these qualities throughout its history, including the so-called period of decline in the seventeenth century. Although the structure of the society changed over time, its outer facade remained intact for at least three centuries. A focus on the outward appearance of the society gives a false sense of continuity. An overly intensive concentration upon outward appearances make it seem as though an old social formation and power structure were still in place, in spite of contemporary evidence showing that major structural changes were in fact occurring. Admittedly, a false impression of continuity can be derived from Ottoman primary sources, which are very much oriented toward the models provided by an idealized past. But a closer inspection re-

veals that contemporary Ottoman writers were not unaware of the changes they witnessed. Some were fully
aware of the changes and simply lamented them; other
writers, like Naima, could not help but accommodate to
change intellectually, even while vigorously defending the
status quo.

In order to understand the insights Ottoman writers of
the seventeenth and eighteenth centuries had about their
society, it is necessary to reconstruct the contemporary
historical context of their writings. Only then can we ap-
preciate the precise meaning and the subtleties of texts
which at first glance read like outright replicas of earlier
works. Modern historians have interpreted the dependence
on precedents as evidence for a lack of innovation, as simple imitation lacking in originality. The matter is far more
complicated, however. As suggested in the present study,
the reproducing of ancient precedents and of an ancient
historiographical point of view by Ottoman authors often
had political implications and social utility for the time in
which these authors were active.

Second, although the state of research in the field of
Ottoman history allows no definitive answers, it is imper-
ative to raise the question why the sociopolitical changes
outlined in the previous pages took place at the time they
did. Considerable economic changes took place in the later
sixteenth century when Mustafa 'Ali was living through
the most active stages of his career: prices rose, probably
both in response to population growth and to the importation of American silver.[66] In addition, demand by nascent
European textile industries pushed up the price of raw silk
and cotton, and even though some Ottoman manufactures
ultimately rallied, the immediate result was a noticeable
economic crisis.[67]

All of these difficulties must have had social repercussions. Their exploration is still very much in its infancy
however, and the results are correspondingly crude and ap-
proximate. It is known that the central treasury's insatia-
ble demand for cash led to the spread of tax farming.
Moreover, provincial governors were increasingly expected

to finance their own retinues of armed men. Locally levied taxes assumed greater importance as did the power of those who were able to take a hand in apportioning the taxes. On their part, tax farmers appointed for short terms often squeezed the taxpayers to such a degree that their long-term ability to pay was jeopardized.[68] At the very end of the seventeenth century this last consideration led to the institution of life-term tax farms, the so-called mali-kane, whose holders, because of their length of tenure, were expected to take an interest in the taxpayers' welfare. In the long run, however, a large number of malikanes threatened the central administration's control over tax revenue. It would be worth investigating how the institution of the malikane may have compounded the tendency toward grandee politics.

The third generalization is central to this study: namely, how best to approach the question of the nature of the Ottoman state in early modern times. To put the matter succinctly, there is an early modern state formation, whose breakdown is characterized by a process of decentralization of power and the abandonment of the early modern, class-bound merit-for-service system.

Up to this point, close examination of the evidence from the second half of the seventeenth century points toward two contradictory interpretations. The first supports the view of a nascent early modern centralizing effort with connotations deceptively similar to the practices of the modern nation-state. This trend is apparent even in the eighteenth century, when central authority is generally considered by twentieth century scholars to have been at its weakest. Initially, the nascent early modern centralization is characterized by the separation of public affairs from the personal affairs of the ruler and his family, the tendency to transform the zone frontier into a demarcated linear border, a growing specialization of function in some branches of the central administration, and finally, by the rapid conversion of public lands into semiprivate property. It may even be argued that the sacred law, the şeri'at, was used to support centralizing tendencies. The accumulated evidence suggests that the Ottoman state was moving rapidly toward an autonomy of the modern type, separating the state from both society and economy.[69]

Other clusters of evidence seem to favor a contradictory interpretation which accords primacy to class and society. I am proposing that the focus on class, and therefore on social formation rather than on the state, will bear more fruitful results. Focusing on class is possible only if at the same time we discuss the relationship between class and state. Primary sources from the sixteenth and seventeenth centuries point to distinctions between the state and the ruling class which must have been functional, since in those years the state served as an extension of the socioeconomic interests of the ruling class. Like other ruling classes, the Ottoman ruling class publicly adhered to the view that the means of production, and therefore the appropriation of surplus, were held in trust by themselves, to be administered and expended for the public good. This attitude was expressed by a formula which called the public treasury the *beytu mali-lmuslimin* (the treasury of the Muslims).

I would argue further that dedication to the public good was, in the final analysis, an ideological posture that justified and allowed the ruling class to regularly assign to itself the surpluses generated by the society at large. Dedication to the public good should therefore be treated as a legitimizing formula, not because many members of the ruling class failed to live up to it, but because the formula was used consistently for making the domination of the ruling class socially acceptable.[70]

At several points in this study I have contrasted the modern and the early modern views of public service. When dealing with primary materials on Ottoman social, political, and economic practices, it is necessary to examine and put in context the contemporary Ottoman attitudes. In the sixteenth and seventeenth centuries, the Ottoman ruling class, like its counterparts elsewhere in Europe, took nepotism and personal influence (intisap) for granted. To obtain public office for family members or for members of one's household, or to arrogate to oneself and to members of one's household great and sometimes fabulous wealth, were considered legitimate practices as long as one belonged to the ruling class. Subscribing to the notion that appointments and benefices should follow the early modern merit system (which, however, was considered applicable only to members of the ruling class), 'Ali and Koçu Bey condemned the later practices as corrupt. Naima and the early eighteenth century memorialist Defterdar Mehmed Paşa disagree. Nor do Ottoman members of the seventeenth century ruling class manifest any sense of wrongdoing, even though twentieth century scholars, following the lead given by authors such as 'Ali and Koçu Bey, consider these behaviors as symptoms of greed, nepotism, and corruption.

To the modern mind, service in the public interest is associated with meritocratic practices, equity, institutional objectivity, and judicial independence. Rationality binds these processes together; all are characteristic of the modern nation-state. By contrast, the Ottoman ruling class made no distinction between personal patrimony and property on the one hand, and the public treasury on the other. Those members of the ruling class who were in power appropriated whatever wealth they could, without any sense of corruption or greed, but rather out of a sense of entitlement. The most often quoted expression of that sanction is found in the "divinely" inspired formula: "Verily He created you into (separate) orders"[71] The notion that these Ottoman practices are an indication of corruption stems from the modern assumption that the public interest is separate from the individual interest of the dominant members of the ruling class. Certainly, it must be admitted that corruption and nepotism were thoroughly condemned by 'Ali and Koçu Bey, and also by later generations of Ottoman writers, whose condemnations, however, were not and could not be based on the standards of the nation-state. Rather, they were predicated on early modern standards of public service and merit, but were distorted by nineteenth and twentieth century scholars who interpreted the Ottoman authors' texts without taking into account the historical occasion for their composition. It may be recalled that rarely if ever did these writers see the revenue-producing classes as anything but providers. Neither mobility nor equality is anywhere tolerated or encouraged. Instead the reaya were expected to remain in their social and economic positions.

The dividing line that separated the personal treasuries of individual members of the ruling class from the public treasury was often tenuous. For example, I cite the Köprülü seventeenth century grandee family or Mustafa II's *şeyhulislam* Feyzullah Efendi, with a talent for accumulating treasures and property. Members of the Köprülü family tried to shelter their wealth from the müsadere or confiscation policy.[72] There is, however, a corollary that can best be described as *noblesse oblige.* Individual grandees committed their individual talents and private wealth (and/or that of their households) to public service. Contrary to what 'Ali and Koçu Bey predicted, even when those who obtained appointment were not members of the military orders, they were expected to, and often did, equip auxiliary troops at their own personal expense. Their civic sense was expressed also by contributing directly to the public treasury when it was short of cash. Thus for example, forty-five officers and officials, including the grand vezir, the janissary *aga,* the grand vezir's deputies (*kaymakams*), and other high-level officials in the capital, contributed a total of one hundred thirty-seven *keses* of *akçes* for the campaign of 1109 (1697–1698).[73]

To further meet their civic responsibilities, members of the ruling class particularly the grandee families and their various allied households endowed pious and philanthropic foundations. These were among the most visible signifiers of the ruling elite's dedication to public welfare. Throughout the Ottoman domains they built elaborate networks of useful institutions: hospitals, mosques, soup kitchens, libraries, schools, colleges, student scholarships, hostels for travelers, and even water fountains for ablutions prior to prayers or for drinking purposes. The Ottoman ruling class's dedication to public welfare and service should not be allowed to mask the ideological uses of their commitment. Rather, their munificence should be interpreted as the necessary sacrifice of a small portion of the elite's personal wealth, which had been derived from the expropriation of surpluses generated by the reaya. These expenditures for the creation, reproduction, replication, and continued support of civic institutions were part of a self-assessment scheme in a socioeconomic system which the class as a whole had a vital interest in preserving.

For the seventeenth and eighteenth centuries, one needs to ask how many mosques, hospitals, schools, and other philanthropic foundations were established by the then dominant elements of the ruling class. Such a breakdown would immediately demonstrate the palace's loss of power in contrast to (the earlier period, that is,) the fifteenth and sixteenth centuries, when several imperial mosques were built, each with an elaborate complex of schools, hospitals, and soup kitchens. In the one hundred fifty or so years after 1607, only three or four large but inexpensively constructed mosques were built by members of the dynasty. For the same period, there is evidence that numerous more modest foundations were endowed by the new members of the ruling elite in Istanbul and throughout the Empire.[74]

In their social commitments, the ruling factions of the Ottoman elite did not differ from their contemporary and near contemporary counterparts in Western Europe. Not only was it their view that resources and wealth were theirs for the taking. They also took responsibility by drawing on their own resources to uphold a system within which, after all, they were the principal beneficiaries.[75]

X.

From the evidence presented up to this point one could conclude that in the seventeenth century an Ottoman

state was in the process of formation, a state in which public functions were gaining ground at the expense of private
and personal interests. This interpretation favors the autonomy of the state formation at the expense of the private
affairs of the ruling class. However, the evidence supports
an opposing interpretation as well. After all, the ruling
class can be perceived as treating the means of production
as its own patrimony, covertly disposing of productive resources as though they were private property, and evolving
an administrative structure to facilitate the performance of
these tasks. These opposite interpretations could be recon-
ciled by designating the early modern period as transitional, and by pointing to a number of contradictory
tendencies.

It is clear that the Ottoman state formation passed
through two distinct phases. The first phase continued
from the mid-fifteenth to the mid-sixteenth century. During this period, the ruling elite by consensus allowed a
limited number of public service appointments based on
merit. By restricting public service to members of the ruling class, the major benefits of the system accrued to those
people who belonged to this same class and who partook
of its culture. Whatever autonomous institutional structures existed were set up by the ruling class to facilitate a
regulated and legitimized exploitation of material and human resources. The second phase, beginning in the late
sixteenth century and proceeding through the seventeenth,
saw the erosion of one consensus within the ruling elite
and the rise of another. The state formation of the first period underwent changes in the face of intensifying competition within the ruling elite for access to resources and
revenues. If it ever existed as an historical phenomenon,
the well-regulated society, with the clearly defined social
orders so much favored by 'Ali and Koçu Bey, had broken
down and ceased to provide insight into the actual social
formations of the day. The second period (from at least the
1560s through the 1700s) is characterized by social mobility, fluidity of practice, and flux in fortunes. Flexibility is
evident even in the application of the şeri'at and the ad

hoc nature of its enforcement. In most instances, the religious law seems to have been tailored to meet the needs of the ruling class whenever its interests demanded such an adjustment.

The focus on class rather than on state provides a better means of evaluating the early modern Ottoman state formation and society. For one thing, it allows research of sociopolitical and socioeconomic questions to proceed without any need to enter into the uncertain and volatile area of theorizing about the so-called Asiatic Mode of Production (AMP).[76] Another advantage is that an emphasis on class frees the modern researcher to study early modern state formation as separate from its modern counterpart, and without projecting onto the early modern period more recently developed, and by now firmly established, concepts and structures found in the modern nation-state. The nation-state comprises, after all, a highly developed and a clearly defined set of bureaucratic and meritocratic practices and institutions. Mixing up the two forms of state scarcely permits a fair evaluation of the performance of Ottoman society as a whole. Finally, an emphasis upon the concept of class allows the researcher to situate the study of early modern Ottoman history in a comparative framework rather than in the prevailing particularist one. From the twentieth century Ottoman historian's point of view, this last is perhaps the most important consideration, for only by comparing the Ottoman early modern social and political formations, with their counterparts in other societies, can sense be made out of them.

Epilogue

The primary research upon which this study is based focused initially on the second half of the seventeenth century and later was extended back in time, to probe the principal trends affecting the nature of state and society in the sixteenth century. In this section I will briefly explore the eighteenth and nineteenth centuries, in order to trace what became of these trends during the modern period. Underlying this effort is my contention that the study of early modern history, specifically, that of the Ottoman Empire, has relevance for the late twentieth and the early twenty-first centuries.

Using the nation-state as an inevitable culmination point in their studies, most scholars of the modern period have used the nineteenth century as a base for understanding the earlier centuries of Ottoman history. Mainstream twentieth century scholarship proclaims the tanzimat period as the historical juncture for the appearance of the modern state which, with its streamlined and seemingly autonomous institutions, was adopted wholesale by the Ottomans. At the same time, a bureaucratic merit system was developed to protect the state's autonomy. Since the procedures, laws, and regulations of the modern state, as developed in Western Europe, were by this time mostly systematized and rationalized, they seemed to transcend the whims of the moment. Moreover, unlike many types of law in other early societies, the law of the nation-state was not seen as simply a system of regulations aimed at facilitating the control of their subjects by the ruling class. It was actually supposed to be enforceable by the state, equally on all citizens, both in its spirit and in its specific provisions.

The prevailing scholarly view of the tanzimat reforms presents major methodological problems. It postulates that the Ottoman reforms of the nineteenth century are based on an external (i.e., Western) model, which was imported and superimposed on Ottoman society. The assumption is that somehow the older system of government and social organization had ceased to regenerate and renew itself. Therefore the changes of the nineteenth century are depicted as sudden and new, indeed, unprecedented. The methodological and scientific problems posed by this view should make the historian gravely sceptical. After all, it implies a fundamental improbability: that Ottoman society was static and that a complete change took place within a short period of time, with virtually no preparation or precedent. Given the usual bias of historians in favor of gradual change, such an assertion should not have been accepted without strong supporting evidence, and a good deal of debate. The exact opposite has occurred, however, and what is astonishing is that the methodological difficulties have, in fact, disturbed few researchers. Thus critical observers are confirmed in their suspicions that most of the research on nineteenth and twentieth century Ottoman history is based on advocacy of specific political propositions, rather than on scientific concerns. Much of the work on the nineteenth century Ottoman Empire starts out from very simple proposition: Ottoman society, being traditional, had no way but to become a modern or better society. The structural form that this transformation took was the nation-state.

By presenting the nation-state as an inevitable outcome of the encounter between early modern and modern society discourages (if it does not actually dismiss as useless) the systematic study of early modern (sometimes called traditional) society, and renders it a waste of time to devote sustained intellectual energies to the analysis of what was, when all is said and done, an "obsolete," "lifeless," and "useless" body.[77] With few exceptions, whatever the secondary literature yields with respect to the background for the reforms of the nineteenth century is based on no actual examination of Ottoman institutions, society, and practices of the preceding two to three hundred years. Until now, serious research on these critical centuries has been at best erratic and unsystematic.[78]

To avoid any misunderstanding about the reasons for stressing the need to study traditional society, I hasten to point out that the motive is not to idealize it. Nor is it my view that there was something inherently good and therefore worth salvaging in traditional society per se. Least of all should my plea for a historical examination of pre-nineteenth century Ottoman history be taken as a campaign in favor of reviving traditional society.

The first task that needs to be emphasized is scholarly: without systematic study of the so-called traditional period of Ottoman history, the assessment of nineteenth century change will remain precarious. Second, the nation-state as a model of social, economic, and political organization has had and continues to cause major problems. In the early 1990s, Western Europe, the founding base for the experiment in nation-state formation, is trying out alternatives as the various national barriers of its several member states are gradually lowered.

It is deplorable that researchers and social thinkers continue to view the nation-state as the pinnacle of early modern Ottoman historical development. Their narrow perspective denies them the many opportunities available to them for first theorizing and then evaluating the potential experiments in multiethnic and multireligious coexistence in the social organization of early modern times as alternate models of social and political organization. As the globe becomes more closely bound in its destiny than ever before, the development of alternative research models becomes all the more urgent. We must research, think, and write less within the parameters of an inevitable but exclusive nationalist model, and more along the lines of an inclusive, universalist culture and society.

Future research in Ottoman history must be guided by the fact that a good part of the meaningful or enduring reforms of the tanzimat represent the culmination of a process of change having roots in the seventeenth century. Beginning in that period and continuing well into the eighteenth century, the Ottoman ruling class experienced a disarticulation that became manifest in part as peasants resisted giving up an increasing share of their production in taxes.[79] The changes in tax collection led to the evolution of a secondary social mechanism in the form of a local ruling elite whose task it was to more directly, systematically, and steadily supervise the collection of taxes, on its own behalf as well as on behalf of the Istanbul-based ruling class. The political result in many regions was the rise of semiautonomous local dynasties. By the later seventeenth and in the eighteenth centuries, the material base of local elites in some regions at least, was dramatically changed by occasional grants of large tracts of land as private property (mülk). In regions where this process was most advanced a good part of miri land was turned into private property. When a bureau of registry for private property was established in the later nineteenth century, it was the end result of a long process of conversion of publicly held lands into de facto private holdings.[80]

In the fifteenth and sixteenth centuries, the Ottoman dynasty interacted with the ruling class of its time in a manner vastly different from the late eighteenth and nineteenth centuries. The difference can be explained by a change in the structure of property-holding. Under the earlier feudal arrangement there was little officially recognized private property; in the later centuries the primary mode of land holding, in practice, took the form of private property. In the earlier mode, the peasant was presumed to be free, possessing the means of production and reproduction; in the eighteenth and nineteenth centuries he was occasionally turned into a source of labor in the service of the ruling class.[81]

The increasing volume of trade had an effect upon the relationship of the Ottoman ruling class to the central state. Certainly, foreign trade had been an important source of revenue ever since the Ottoman Empire had become a world power, and during the sixteenth century, Ottoman Muslim merchants, contrary to widespread belief, had themselves traded in Europe, particularly in Italy.[82] But in the seventeenth and eighteenth centuries, the number of direct commercial transactions between several Ottoman provinces and the outside world increased considerably. Some transactions were carried out legitimately with the consent of Istanbul; others, such as the smuggling of grain and certain raw materials, were illegal. Various ways of sidestepping regulations and avoiding taxes continued even with the formal inauguration of modern-style centralization through the tanzimat.[83] Thus whether through increased control of the peasantry or through profits from foreign trade, the Ottoman provincial elite of the eighteenth and early nineteenth centuries achieved considerable independence from the central authority.

The growing complexity and sophistication in diplomatic and commercial practices suggests an ongoing process of modern centralization by the time the tanzimat reforms were inaugurated. It is possible that some of the tanzimat reforms represented mere changes in labels, or that they were the result of a continuous process dating back at least two hundred years. In other words, the tanzimat can be seen, in part, as the synthesis of a two hundred year sequence of experiments and ad hoc solutions. The process was by no means unilinear and uninterrupted; quite the contrary, there were marked setbacks, especially in the processes of centralization and modern state formation.

Late seventeenth and eighteenth century official transactions recorded in the so-called Registers of Important Affairs (mühimme defterleri) support the hypothesis that modern centralization, as institutionalized during the tanzimat, really had its beginnings in earlier centuries. As early as the later sixteenth and seventeenth centuries, these documents testify to a narrowing specialization of functions within the Ottoman central administration. Why some specialized functions developed earlier than others is a matter that needs further study.[84] I contend that specialization of function preceded the tanzimat by several centuries and served internal Ottoman needs at particular junctures in time. It is, therefore, not the European models for change that gave rise to the development of the tanzimat. Rather the change was inaugurated by one stratam of Ottoman society and benefited the Ottoman ruling class.

The office of the reisülküttap (chief of secretaries in the grand vezir's office) in the seventeenth and eighteenth centuries may serve as an example of the development of modern centralization and modern bureaucratic practices. A comparative study of similar offices in Western Europe and the United States at about the same time would reveal that far from being unique, the evolution of the office of the reisülküttap conformed to patterns of development discernible in comparable offices within other bureaucracies. A comparative study of the nearly contemporary institutions of European foreign ministries and of the United States Department of State shows parallel historical developments. The office of the reisülkütap started as an executive secretariat, which, like the Department of State, shed over time many of its purely secretarial functions and became focused mainly on foreign affairs.[85] Already by the seventeenth century, officers in this position were called upon to serve as Ottoman representatives in diplomatic negotiations. The trend continued into the eighteenth century. By then, the office of reisülküttap experienced further structural changes to accommodate new functions and requirements, added in response to further changes in the diplomatic position of the Ottomans. In addition, some of the bureaucratic changes were meant to allow the Ottoman central administration to cope more effectively with newly concluded trade agreements, such as the arrangements to facilitate trade with the Habsburg Empire.[86]

The above interpretation contradicts the view that changes in the role of the reisülküttap were part and parcel of an Ottoman attempt to accomodate the requirements of modernization in the nineteenth century. According to the latter view, an Ottoman ministry of foreign affairs was adopted deliberately in order to provide an institutional counterpart to the European office. The rationale behind the counter-argument presented here is that hardly any new institution was adopted wholesale; rather, offices in the Ottoman administration evolved over time as a result of internal needs for bureaucratic specialization. Therefore, the history of Ottoman bureaucracy in general, and the office of reisülküttap in particular, must be studied through the analysis of institutional practices as they evolved over a period of two centuries.

Since the case is being made here for the internal roots rather than the external cause of the tanzimat reforms, it may be useful to place political change in a broader social and cultural context. Where the eighteenth century is concerned, there is a discernible increase in interest by the Ottoman ruling elite in developments outside the Ottoman realm, so much so that one can almost speak of a kind of cultural symbiosis between the Ottoman ruling class and the elites of several southeastern European states. This cultural symbiosis has attracted most attention in the context of eighteenth century baroque Ottoman architecture.[87] Perhaps more significant are changes in thinking with regard to daily life.

Daniel Panzac has pointed out that by the later eighteenth century, some members of the Ottoman elite had given up the belief that epidemics were an act of God to which human beings could only submit, and were instead actively proposing, and later enforcing, quarantine measures.[88] Now the Ottoman elite had been aware of European attitudes in this regard for several centuries, for European merchants and diplomats residing in the Ottoman Empire had practiced quarantine throughout the sixteenth and seventeenth centuries. That the Ottoman elite became receptive to the practice of quarantine in the eighteenth century, and not before, indicates that it was the elite's own needs which determined its response, and not the mere physical presence of European models. Similarly, it is of some significance that early in the eighteenth century, the central administration instituted the testing and licensing in the capital of surgeons and doctors among both European and local practitioners.[89] A similar point could be made with respect to the adoption of landscape painting as a decoration in wealthy Ottoman houses, and also with regard to the changes in the Ottoman bureaucracy referred to above.

The present study is based upon two assumptions: first, that the Ottoman elite throughout its history was in some contact with Europe—there never was an "iron curtain" blocking the exchange of new ideas; and second, that the adoption of cultural patterns, whether from Europe or elsewhere, was not simply the result of a foreign presence, nor was it just an emulation of an attractive outside model: it was determined by the needs of the Ottoman ruling elite.

In reviewing the common features of the differences between early modern and modern forms of centralization, the early nineteenth century, and the peculiar tensions which filled the reign of Mahmud II (1808–1839) are of special interest. Beginning in the late eighteenth century, and more particularly in the early nineteenth, some sectors in the Ottoman ruling class showed an inclination to return the reigning dynasty to its former position as a dominant element within the ruling class. When the future "father" of the tanzimat, Mahmud II, was besieged by his enemies, it was the aid of some members of the provincial noble elite, and especially Bayrakdar/Alemdar Mustafa Paşa that saved him. The rapprochement between the sultan and ruling elite was uneven and never without ambivalence. Given these limitations, however, the impression remains that some groups among the provincial notables and a sector of the centrally based power-holding elite were willing to cooperate for the purpose of strengthening the Ottoman dynasty.

It is in this light that the final abandonment of decentralization and the thrust for a modern form of centralization should be examined. Some notables must have expected to control, however indirectly, the new-style centralization. A measure of their failure can be seen in Mahmud II's nearly successful experiment to create an autonomous state.[90] Undoubtedly, the dissension among members of the Ottoman ruling elite contributed to the sultan's somewhat unexpected victory.

The centralization instituted by Mahmud II differed from its early modern counterpart of the sixteenth century, for it presumed a state formation that would tackle not only external problems, such as defense and direct competition with the outside world, but also major internal problems, derived in part from fragmentation of power and in part from military and economic interventions by European states.

The potential advantages of a modern-style centralization for the commercial and economic interests of the Ottoman ruling classes of the day were obvious. Among other things, centralization secured communications, transportation, and preventive health measures. Throughout the world these features form part and parcel of a rationalized capitalist state formation that aims at the maximization of profit by capitalist entrepeneurs. In the late nineteenth and early twentieth centuries, the Ottoman state came to resemble this model of state formation ever more, as successive governments tried, albeit with little success, to protect local products and markets from external competition. This protection partially explains the surrender of their autonomy by the local elites. The nineteenth century Ottoman state took on other characteristics of the modern state, including a new ideology, Ottomanism, an uneasy mix of the old ideology (Ottoman culture and Islam) and modern nationalism.[91] In the early twentieth century some Ottoman cultural elements and Islamic elements were abandoned in favor of Turkism, a more potent device based on an ethnic identity and dependent on a language-based nationalism.

The transformation of the Ottoman state in the course of the nineteenth century took place not without occasional fierce struggles among different sectors of the ruling group, some based in the capital and others in the provinces. It is too early to conclude whether in the course of centralization a sector of the ruling class was created that possessed a definite stake in the autonomy of the state, or whether centralization was used mainly as a tool which those members of the ruling class who sat at the levers of power used to disqualify their rivals. Be that as it may, there was no consensus within the ruling class on the course to be taken. In certain areas, the disagreement appeared as a clash between locally based socioeconomic forces and the central state, with its capacity to regulate trade and production. The case of southern Iraq in the nineteenth century is but one example.[92] Throughout that century merchants and producers in this region were involved in a regional marketing system that tied them to the economies of eastern Arabia on the one hand, and southwestern Iran on the other. In order to redirect trade flows in conformity to demands from Istanbul, the Ottoman central administration attempted to "discipline the market" by political intervention. The attempt was met with widespread resistance.

The precariousness of the new Ottoman state is demonstrated by its inability to tap the wealth of its own domains. Instead, the state turned to external sources for military and financial support in its bid for autonomy and centralization. This policy facilitated a sustained attempt by Mahmud II and his immediate successors to experiment with the creation of an autonomous state. The sultan used Western support in his struggle against Mehmed Ali of Egypt, while later rulers relied on the infusion of foreign capital in the form of loans. (There was only a theoretical possibility, obviously not realized, that the Ottoman state could have tapped its own resources following a social revolution.) The dependence on outside support has been replicated by modern Turkey, whose reliance on foreign investments and capital increases in proportion to its reluctance and growing inability to effect revolutionary socioeconomic change. Turkey's dependence on external capitalist investment was intended to forestall radical internal reforms. All external investment has achieved, however, is to postpone the day of reckoning. The result has been internal strife, with all the characteristics of a civil war. Since the end of World War II, each major civil outbreak in Turkey has been met by increasingly harsh military intervention. The consequences of the escalating violence are difficult to foresee.

The oil producing Near Eastern states that succeeded the Ottoman Empire display a myopia similar to that of the successive governments of modern Turkey. In the Turkish case, foreign sources of revenue have allowed the modern state virtual autonomy and the illusion that it is exempt from the consent of the taxed. On the other hand, the oil producing countries have secured no popular consensus with respect to the shape the future is to take. In lieu of a consensus, the ruling classes superimpose modernization unilaterally and finance it out of "unearned" oil revenue. In the meantime, the older economies on which the social formations were once founded have ceased to function. The most basic needs, including basic food products which at one time had been met by the traditional economy, are now met by imports. An early modern parallel easily comes to mind: Spain during the sixteenth and seventeenth centuries also used unearned capital from the New World to meet its basic needs and to import manufactured goods. The dependence upon imports in turn led to a neglect of the local economy comparable to that witnessed today in the oil producing countries. Thus the power of a centralized state, along with the reliance upon unearned income, which the existence of the Spanish Empire made possible, placed Spanish society in a more dependent position economically than it had been at any other time in its history.[93]

Political change in the nineteenth century Ottoman Empire had a social and economic basis. No single individual, neither Sultan Mahmud II nor anyone else, should be considered as the sole initiator of change. Moreover, political change depended not only on external pressures, such as European commercial and economic competition, and even more directly, on military threats on the part of the

Great Powers. Quite the contrary: the forces crucial in bringing about change were internal, reflecting the interests of a section of the ruling class which considered political change as advantageous to itself. Without the presence of such a group, it is unlikely that the Ottoman state would have survived into the twentieth century.[94]

From the methodological point of view, perceiving political change in the light of economic and social interests requires a different kind of research program for the study of Ottoman history. Instead of focusing exclusively on the foreign policies of the major European powers and treating the Ottoman Empire as a dependent variable, this approach requires the analysis of the internal dynamics of Ottoman society from the late sixteenth through the nineteenth century. In addition, the research agenda allows scholars to block out specific chronological periods whose limits are defined by both internal and external dynamic factors. Future research will require testing the scientific viability of the propositions for each specified time period, and enable scholars to better understand the dynamics of the Ottoman social formation.[95]

Afterword

Theorizing Beyond the Nation-State

Histories written in the twentieth century that dealt with the early modern period and the last century of Ottoman history shared the premise that the nation-state is the culmination of the historical process. Indeed, the nation-state was perceived by some scholars as inevitable, even predestined. In the 1950s, modernization advocates claimed that if a society did not voluntarily modernize— that is, Westernize—that process would be forced upon it. It might even represent, as some would still have it, the end of history![96] However, there are alternatives: illustrations can be drawn, for example, from Chinese and Indian history, and from the "middle centuries" (ca. 1580s to 1800) of the history of Ottoman society.

The first and last periods of Ottoman history are historiographically and thematically tied together, through conquest and reconquest by *gazi* warriors. In the first period, the process of conquest began about 1300; in the second, the *gazi*s were represented in the person of Mustafa Kemal Atatürk. The early modern Ottoman period and the last 150 years share a fixation on the power and structure of the state—and especially on its role in conquest—that often amounted to obsession.

Given these historiographical assumptions concerning

the earliest and the latest periods of Ottoman history, I would argue against the paradigm of the nation-state as the inevitable issue of modern history, and against its corollary, the demise of history. I contend that the nation-state should instead be viewed simultaneously as representing a transitional object and as one of several choices for political organizing during set historical junctures. These choices mirror the interests of diverse social forces in their struggle for power in late Ottoman history. Such a methodological approach, emphasizing the existence of alternatives at critical junctures in history, is gaining currency as part of an urgent research agenda among a small scholarly circle in Middle Eastern studies.[97]

Against the nation-state paradigm, it is appropriate today to put forth a research agenda that will guide our examination of options in writing the history of the twenty-first century, a task that clearly has serious implications for modern times. A weakening of national sovereignty in various regions appears to be sending the world into two diametrically opposite directions of consolidation and fragmentation. On the one hand, in Europe (particularly Western Europe), the substantial weakening of national sovereignty created by the evolution of the European Union appears to be spurring the region toward some kind of union. On the other hand, weakened national sovereignty in other parts of the globe seems to be leading to new or broadened divisions that express intolerance for cultural diversity, whether in the form of hatred of national minorities or as insidious racism. This alternate trend is particularly apparent in eastern and southeastern Europe, the countries formerly forming part of or subordinate to the Soviet Union, and many parts of Asia and Africa.[98] Yet in the middle of the display of cultural symbiosis and diversity in the European Union, it is perhaps ironic that division in the form of racism seems to be growing, as illustrated especially by hostility toward Africans, Arabs, and Muslims.[99] Such racism is spelled out in the social policy instituted in England to discipline its Muslim minority (as became obvious during the Rushdie affair) and in calls for the explusion of Arabs from France, as adumbrated by Jean-Marie Le Pen.

In evidence of the second trend—toward fragmentation—we cite cases from the once seemingly intact ethnic
republics of the former USSR, now in some cases apparently
united into a very loose confederation of independent states.
Other examples can be found in the breakup of Yugoslavia,
the disintegration of Lebanon, the struggle in Israel/Pales-
tine, the threats posed to Hungarians in Rumanian Transyl-
vania, and the insecure status of Albanians in Yugoslavia, as
well as in the form of anti-Turkism—most recently, though
briefly, in Bulgaria.[100]

A good number of the national entities outside Western
Europe experiencing this drift toward fracture share certain
common features, most notably the fact that most happen
to be creations of international agreements, imposed either
at the end of World War I or after World War II. All were created as a result of political accommodations imposed by one
ethnic group at the expense of others. More specifically,
they share equally the imposition of an ill-fitting homogeneity on societies composed of highly differentiated identities. The example of Yugoslavia is perhaps the most
paradigmatic. This state was created after World War I by a
union of several distinct ethnic groups, notably Bosnians,
Croats, and Serbs, with the Serbs dominating. The union
was threatened during World War II, but was patched up by
the end of the war only to fall apart in the 1990s.

The recent tendency toward political fragmentation
seems to display, nearly consistently, one clear two-stage
pattern. The first stage is characterized by a tendency to
back away from homogeneity of any sort and the second by
a threat of secession as a prelude to outright independence.
Abstractly, this pattern appears first as a step backward, toward a demand for total sovereignty based on autarchy—a
paradoxical position since autarchy is impossible to achieve
even for the globe's materially and socially best-endowed
nation-states.[101] Thus, in the euphoria of self-assertion and
the haste for outer recognition of one's ethnic identity, the
end of national sovereignty represents, relatively speaking,
a regression, as social groups forced into the political structures created after World Wars I and II react by calling for
separation and independence. For a great number of these

same groups, the end of the twentieth century provided the first historical occasion to assert their respective "national" identities.

Ironically, however, once conditions for recognition as a separate national entity have been fulfilled, a slight shift in the angle of approach often spurs a trend in the opposite direction, as the now sovereign groups seem inclined toward a voluntary return into the fold of some larger community of states, including those from which they had only recently separated. Unlike the earlier polities imposed on these groups from outside, however, this new shift toward consolidation represents a voluntary reentry, including curtailment of several aspects of sovereignty, as illustrated by the European Union.[102]

In the last decade of the twentieth century, it became apparent that political events had caught up with the ongoing academic and political discourses on the nature of the modern state, its historicity, and its viability as a form or model for political organization. Alternative paradigms to the nation-state were proposed, whether in the form of a suprastate formation (such as the European Union), a confederation of (nearly) equal political entities (like the Swiss confederation), or some other loosely integrated form of common market. As stated earlier, my objective in this study is to raise the possibility of political forms forming alternatives to the model of the nation-state that evolved in early modern times, especially between 1500 and 1800 in Ottoman society and elsewhere. In light of the experience of several societies from early modern times, we should ask ourselves what forms of political and social organization will become available in the twenty-first century. For all those concerned about the future of mankind, it is important to initiate the process of thinking and theorizing about the historical roots of ongoing and future experiments in social and political organization.

Beginning as early as 1400, Ottoman historiography has emphasized expansion through territorial conquest rather than through acculturation and assimilation. This applies to the population of Anatolia in the former Byzantine Empire as well as to the various ethnic groups of the Balkans after the Ottoman conquest.[103]

Especially for some modern Turkish scholars, the clear attraction of the Ottoman formative period as a topic for study derives from the fact that it was a time of triumph and expansion, making it an impressive background against which to construct the history of the modern Turkish Republic. The prime advocate of this approach is Ö. L. Barkan.[104]

Barkan and some of his fellow nationalist historians tend to skip over the period between the 1580s and the 1800s, which they regard as lacking the qualities that make a worthy subject of study. This oversight is typical of a type of historiography that intentionally recasts the past for ideological purposes, as Eric Hobsbawm has shown.[105] The controversy surrounding the National Socialist era of German historiography constitutes another example of this ideological approach.[106] An investigation of historical and social scientific writings on the Ottoman period of Arab history, written in Arabic and published between 1952 and 1990, suggests a similar pattern of social use.[107] Here the crucial centuries between 1516 and 1919 are defined simply as a period of "decline" and ignored, because during this period Arabs lived under foreign rule. However, it seems unlikely that Arab history can be written without accounting for nearly four hundred years of life under Ottoman sultans.

The first two centuries of the Ottoman state are probably less important for the history of the empire than the developments of later years. A discourse centered on conquest obeys, falsely, the logic of making the smaller part stand for the whole; the themes of *gazi*dom and territorial expansion are made into the standard by which to assess the remainder of Ottoman history. Since the years between 1580 and 1800 lacked the characteristics of dynamic territorial expansion, they are found wanting. The distortion caused by this historiographic bias is also, in part, a product of modern historians' colonial, hegemonic, and imperial fascination with militarism, conquest, and expansion. The current focus on the early Ottoman state can be attributed to the affinity of these same scholars to military history, as a reflection of their own hegemonic approach to the study of West Asia.[108]

Modern Turkish historians often tend to regard the period 1800–1920 as a prelude to the Turkish Republic, contrasting the attempts to reclaim territory in these years with the several dozen decades of "salutary neglect" and the splintering of the empire's central authority, as illustrated by the rise of the *ayan* dynasties from among the provincial notables late in the seventeenth and in the eighteenth centuries.[109] The first serious attempt at slowing the evolution of the empire toward a loose federation of autonomous states comes with Western-inspired modern centralism, reproduced in the form of the Tanzimat-instituted hegemony during the 1830s.

From an early twentieth-century perspective, there is logic in the argument in favor of such a culmination of the historical process. Before the disappearance of the Ottoman Empire after World War I, several features of the modern nation-state were already in place, created by developments in Ottoman society over the previous two centuries. Attempts at reconquest allowed the Ottomans—unlike the colonizing, imperial European nation-states of the time—to exercise a new sovereignty over territories that had previously acquired a substantial measure of autonomy. Ali Ahmida's 1990 study showed that in the nineteenth century and the early years of the twentieth, the Ottoman state pursued a policy that was "nationalist" in ardor, to retain and reclaim the Libyan provinces. Ahmida describes the sultan's proclaimed sovereignty over Cyrenaica and Tripolitania. At the time, the Ottoman claim was contested by Italy, on the grounds that these Ottoman provinces once had been a Roman imperial possession.[110]

The process of nationalist invention, started in the Tanzimat period, was intensified by the Young Turks. Regardless of ethnic and confessional background, all who entered the newly formed public education system were to be instructed in Ottoman Turkish. By the beginning of World War I the Turkification of a significant number of non-Turks, usually of humble origins, had been achieved. (For example, my father, born in 1900, was required to study

Arabic, his native tongue, as a foreign language; all other instruction at his school in Jerusalem was given in Ottoman Turkish.) Had this process of education endured for at least two more generations, it would have created a whole new class of Turkish-speaking subjects who could have contributed to the survival of the late Ottoman state in whatever territories it might have managed to retain. That the Young Turk policies were ultimately and fatefully meant to lead to a homogeneous and binding nationalist loyalty is illustrated by the fate of some of the separatists, both Arab and Armenian, who were punished with public hanging.

The outcome of the political process that portended the creation of a homogenous society with an Ottoman Turkish culture did not preclude different alternatives to the nation-state. In the latter half of the nineteenth century, options were debated. One was offered by a group of intellectuals, the Young Ottomans, whose political agenda incorporated different cultures and confessional groups. Another such option is only discerned from the debates that preceded the adoption of a Western-style constitution in 1876.

With these few exceptions Ottoman political culture has been ignored by the scholarship concerning the nineteenth century. Here I can only delineate some aspects of the evidence.

About the middle of the nineteenth century, two tracts of the type known as *nasihatname,* or "mirror to princes," were printed for public dissemination. No scholarly work to date has concerned itself with the reason why these tracts were republished at this particular time. Hardly anyone has analyzed the *nasihatname* genre as the main medium for political discussion during at least two hundred years of Ottoman history, bringing out the historical specificity of this type of literature. Most of the time, this genre has been conflated with Islamic culture in general, with the result that it has not entered into the discourse concerning Ottoman political culture. It would be instructive, for example, to examine the analogies, concepts and language of the *nasihatnameler* literature, which must have served as the medium for expressing political discourse.[111]

One of the treatises published was written by Koçu Bey

in the first half of the seventeenth century, with particular focus on the "rights of the *sipahi*" (Ottoman Turkish feudal cavalry). The revival of this medieval class was not really advocated by the polemicists of the nineteenth century. The *sipahi*'s rights were merely used as an example of what Ottoman rights in the constitution should be, much as the Magna Carta is evoked in English political rhetoric. (In the nineteenth century edition of Koçu Bey's treatise, the marginalia support such a reading, as we find there two Arabic proverbs: "an hour of justice does more good than seventy years of religious devotion;" and "the master of a people is their servant, and the servant of the people is their master."][112]

Because of its nationalist orientation, the scholarly literature has obscured the experimental nature and multitude of models for new forms of social and political organization reflected in these tracts. It is only by leaving out the various other options that were discussed at the time of the debate over constitution making, that the selection of the European model appears as foreordained.

In contrast, I will examine three scholarly works, published in the 1960s. In a 1962 study on Ottoman political culture, Şerif Mardin hints at engagement in a multiplicity of discourses, but his monograph focuses mainly on the one developed by the Young Ottomans, early in the second half of the nineteenth century. It is his major concern to follow the threads of evidence leading to the discourse over modernization and the establishment of the Turkish nation-state.[113]

Robert Devereux and Roderic Davison chiefly focus their studies on the adopted Ottoman constitution. They both reach the conclusion that Ottoman society was incapable of accomodating a liberal constitution.[114] The society's diversity, the multitude of ethnic and confessional groups, they argue, was to blame. There is something of an ironic twist to this approach. Although they are both Americans, neither Devereux nor Davison sees any parallel between Ottoman constitution making and its chronological coincidence with the constitutional crisis which resulted in the American civil war. Although U.S. society was guided by a constitution which guaranteed equality to all citizens, the African-American sector of that society had been left out of the political equation. A century later, at about the time the authors' books were published, namely in the 1960s, the civil rights movement challenged the continued existence of this particular divide in U.S. society. When comparing the study of Ottoman society with that of its U.S. counterpart, we discover an amnesia that seemes to have blocked the two authors' historical vision.[115]

In current historiography, it is assumed that modernity is associated with the nineteenth-century nation-state. It is my contention that our historical understanding of Ottoman social and political history in the "middle centuries" (1580s–1800) is badly distorted, because we have become accustomed to assess all change in accordance with standards set by modernization. This paradigm for change has prevailed in the studies focused on the last century of Ottoman rule, and by extension in all West Asian and North African studies.[116]

In the following pages I discuss briefly, without giving primacy to any single factor, certain phenomena indicative of the metamorphoses registered in Ottoman society in the "middle centuries." Among them we might name the wider distribution of wealth across Ottoman society, confirmed by the general growth in urban population, the enlargment of regional markets, and the spatial expansion of cities and towns. All this has been illustrated by recent scholarship on the Arab provinces and the Ottoman capital, as well as on the Balkans. This new scholarship has confirmed the appearance of markets with growing independent wealth in the eighteenth and nineteenth centuries. Hala Fattah's work on the Basra-based regional market, for example, indicates that although the market was centered in Basra, it extended into the Arabian Peninsula to the west and into southwestern Iran to the east and also encompassed overseas trade both across the Gulf and into India.[117] Dina Rizk Khoury likewise has shown a thriving regional market centered in northern Iraq at Mosul.[118] André Raymond's research on the

Arab cities during the Ottoman era suggests similar patterns, although he is reluctant to pinpoint an exact time for the growth in population, wealth, and urban centers during the "middle centuries."[119] Unlike Fattah and Khoury, Raymond attaches no special significance to the later eighteenth-century growth in social and material wealth, simply insisting that growth was apparent and steady from the beginning of Ottoman rule.[120]

For evidence of these transformations in Istanbul, Tülay Artan, an architectural historian, has traced wealth and its diffusion to the rise of new social classes in the eighteenth century, as demonstrated by urban growth and development in the capital's newly created and expanded suburbs. The expansion was especially evident in the numerous investments being made in the new seaside *yalıs* (palaces), resort homes of various sizes and of varying and new styles to match the taste of the new classes that emerged in the "middle centuries" of Ottoman history.[121]

As already indicated, I want to make the case for a transformative process prior to the nineteenth and twentieth centuries. Scholars in other areas have postulated transformations of a similar kind in China and India that correspond to the "middle period" of Ottoman history.[122] In the Ottoman case, we are beginning to identify the phenomenon. From the perspective of the twentieth century, the social, economic, and political experiments of the period displayed two simultaneous but opposing trends: on the one hand, centralization at and managed by the center, on the other, "salutary neglect" and decentralization amounting to virtual autonomy for the provinces. Given the demands of the time and the goals set for the society by the elites of these earlier centuries, these discrepant trends, rather than pulling the society apart, permitted, in a paradoxical fashion, the survival of both the outer framework and the structures of Ottoman society.

By the end of the eighteenth century conditions were rapidly changing, and with external (especially European) threats becoming more direct, the advantages of the trend toward decentralization were outweighed by growing disadvantages. The latter resulted from the model of the nation-state first developed in Western Europe but spreading rapidly into the eastern Mediterranean. The balance between the simultaneous trends toward centralization and decentralization, which once had helped to preserve the territorial integrity of the empire, in the early nineteenth century seemed to lead toward rapid dismemberment. This source of weakness is apparent from the nineteenth-century bids for autonomy or outright independence on the part of Mehmed Ali of Egypt, after help had been provided to the Greeks in their war of independence by the Western powers and the Serbs had achieved similar results. These circumstances early in the nineteenth century compelled certain sectors of the Ottoman ruling class to impose direct control over the provinces. It is within this context that we should view the structural transformations of the Tanzimat, which ultimately were to lead to the creation of a Turkish nation-state. Thus the transformations occurring within Ottoman society from the beginning of the nineteenth century and particularly in the course of the Tanzimat reforms must be viewed, in part, as representing social options advanced from within Ottoman society in reaction to the Western onslaught. The threat from European powers interrupted the gradual emergence of an Ottoman version of sociopolitical transformation, whose end product we can only imagine.

Let us explore some of the other features characteristic of early Ottoman transformation. Perhaps the most fascinating are the halfway solutions, which in retrospect may appear as wild, inexplicable, and even bizarre cultural and social experiments. To a twenty-first-century mind, these solutions surface as an incongruous fusing of opposites, a baroque blend of wild and sometimes exaggerated experiments intended to propitiate seemingly incompatible and irreconcilable social and cultural opposites. Thus against all odds, we witness leaps over the once-unfathomable social, cultural, and indeed aesthetic divides that formerly separated individuals into discrete confessional, ethnic, and linguistic groups. In this manner, new artistic and architectural idioms were created.

On the social level these solutions included bridges over the tabooed confessional divides which suggest that for those who converted Ottoman society retained its credibility. As the first piece of evidence I would mention the spontaneous mass conversions of certain Christian villagers to Islam late in the seventeenth century. The fluidity involved here is not exceptional, and other, different forms of conversion are also on record. In Anatolia in the same century, for example, we have evidence of Western, Catholic proselytizing among the Greek Orthodox and Armenians, echoed as a complaint in the central Ottoman archival registers known as the Mühimme defterleri. It is not the motives or the goals of the Western missionaries that are at issue here, but the openness to conversion evidenced by certain Christian subjects of the sultan.

For outsiders, the most celebrated, but perhaps also the most misunderstood, social phenomenon of this kind is the story of the dönme, a group of converts from Judaism to Islam. Conversion was occasioned in the seventeenth century by the appearance of the Jewish missionary prophet Sabbatai Zvi. His adherents had come into conflict with the "orthodox" Jewish establishment, and protests were lodged against Sabbatai at the Ottoman court. In order to avoid disruption of the social status quo represented by the religious estates—the millets, where each confessional order was preserved as separate from the others—the sultan offered Sabbatai Zvi a choice of either forfeiting his life or accepting Islam. The visionary chose the latter course, and carried with him a considerable number of his followers. The dönme—converts, like the conversos in Spain during the Reconquista—continued to practice their faith in secret. It is hardly possible, however, that the Ottoman authorities did not know of the "dissimulation" practiced by the converts. After the initial act of crossing over into the Muslim community, the converts used their dönme status as a bridge, allowing them movement across social boundaries in both directions, uninhibited by circumstance or time. Their survival into the twenty-first century, however, cannot be taken merely to illustrate the members' tenacity in upholding their Jewish—albeit heretical—heritage, as is emphasized in much of the scholarly literature. Gershom Scholem, one of the latest biographers of Sabbatai Zvi, equally has regarded a rich and complicated story from this narrow viewpoint.

Socially the *dönme* path served as a way to accomodate change without disturbing the culture at large. One can ponder the contrast in historical circumstances and conditions that allowed the survival of this community in present-day Turkey, when juxtaposed against the fate of an analogous group of *conversos*. Initially, during the early Reconquista, Muslims and Jews in Spain had been allowed a similar cover. But in their case, the state later resorted to a final solution of mass expulsion, perceiving Christian homogeneity as the better course to centralization and regarding the subtle heterogeneity of the recanters' conscience as a threat. Typically, perhaps, the sincerity of the converts was always held in doubt.

Less than two centuries later, the Spanish approach to social engineering was reenacted in France, when a military campaign was mounted against the Huguenots. Within a couple of decades following the erection of the *dönme* social bridge, the protection accorded the Protestant dissidents by the Edict of Nantes, signed late in the sixteenth century, was revoked on October 18, 1685. This event parallels the expulsion of the Jewish Marranos and Muslim Moriscos from Spain a century earlier. In the case of the *conversos* and Huguenots, Spain and France combined Catholicism with dynastic loyalty as the foci of both homogeneity and centralization. Before the rise of nationalism, however, as early as the seventeenth century, Ottoman society provided a protective umbrella for experimentation with coexistence and heterogeneity.

Other provisional social metamorphoses surface as trends in social and economic transformation during the two centuries of the Ottoman "middle period." This time, they appear among Greeks and Armenians, as well as among South Slavs in the Ottoman provinces, who engaged in commerce, especially in the Balkan cities. In discussing this phenomenon, Stoianovitch has pointed out that as a result of the growing reliance by Ottoman society on these ethnic groups and the ensuing competition within the new merchant economy of the early modern period, the Jewish merchants lost ground. It is perhaps significant that this development overlapped the rise of Sabbatai Zvi's movement and the eventual conversion of his followers to Islam. Unlike other Jews, the relatively small number of *dönme* were allowed to enter trade alongside the Greeks and Armenians. The *dönme* path thus provided a cultural bridge allowing ostensible Muslims to continue as merchants, while conserving their Jewish identity.[123]

With respect to the early period (1300 to 1580s) and the last century of the empire (1800 to 1918), Ottoman historiography is focused especially on segregation and social separation. In the first centuries we encounter a focus on segregation by confessional groups. In the later period sharp "national" differentiation comes into its own, based on a homogeneous ethnicity and accompanied by growing hostility to social pluralism and heterogeneity.

In the "middle period," in contrast, one can observe the lowering of social barriers of practically every kind, especially in urban environments. Although the trends for change were not pervasive and did not affect all elements in society, they nevertheless reflected a relative growth in economic and social benefits across confessional, ethnic, and linguistic divides.[124]

The shift away from a feudal economy was also reflected in the development of a new social formation. In the urban centers, the entry of members of religious and ethnic minorities into public service was one trend that paralleled the appearance of something resembling secularism in the society at large, and a tacit, but nevertheless relatively significant trend toward equality. In other words, the shift in the economy toward commercialization was accompanied by a shift in the social status of certain sectors in Ottoman society. The feudal *timar*-based economy had corresponded to a hierarchical society, based on religious affiliation and identity and involving segregation. By contrast, the commercialized economy, accompanied by the appearance of private property in various guises, indicated a shift in society that blurred once-clear social distinctions. As noted earlier, these shifts are registered in a literature of polemics that came to serve as the basis for a new political culture in the "middle centuries."[125]

In the Ottoman case, we have already noted that the shift from "salutary neglect" to a new form of centralization coincided with a threat perceived as a destructive external assault in the form of an impinging "world market."[126] On the social structural level, this shift appeared as a collision between two models for the organization of Ottoman polity and society. In the historiography, it is categorized, falsely, as a struggle between tradition, represented by all of Ottoman history prior to 1800, and modernity. However, I propose here that it is more fruitful to see it as a discourse that reflects a struggle between two parallel options for organizing society and polity. Perhaps conveniently for certain researchers, the rubric "tradition" has obscured the various experiments in social and cultural transformation experienced by Ottoman society in the "middle period."

The Ottoman model forged bridges across cultural and social gaps, a process already set in motion by the seventeenth and eighteenth centuries. This social formation managed to accommodate the diversity of the various heterogeneous groups composing the society as whole. Although its logical implications were not apparent early in the nineteenth century, the nation-state model aimed at an opposite social formation, predicated on cultural and ethhic homogeneity, as set forth in its extreme form later on by the Young Turks.

Conceptually, I am proposing to bring back into the historical discourse the seemingly contradictory but transformative social processes of the "middle centuries." This should allow revision of the research agenda for the last four hundred years of Ottoman history. For example, Ottoman history from 1600 onward could be conceptualized more efficaciously as representing a conflict or a choice between at least two models of social and political organization. This clash set the tone for various political and social struggles which made up the history of the last one hundred years of Ottoman rule. Initially, Ottoman society seems to have tolerated the simultaneous functioning of the competing models of centralization and regional autonomy. It is worth noting that the inherent contradiction between the two courses did not result in social paralysis.

The Ottoman version of change as it evolved in the "middle period" was not unique in the world of its time. We may regard it as an experiment that not only tolerated but actually encouraged nearly full participation in the economy and society on the part of diverse ethnic and confessional groups. For some elements of Ottoman society, the process transformed the dominant culture, which now contained such hybrids as Ottoman-Armenian and Ottoman-Jewish literatures. In a similar fashion, Ottoman Turkish as a language affected the Arabic dialect, particularly in the area we call Palestine but in other Arab provinces as well. Only in the second half of the nineteenth century did the adoption of the nation-state as a model for modernity began to cancel out the development of a social order accommodating cultural, ethnic, and confessional diversity. These are the very characteristics, it may be recalled, that distinguish the agenda for transformation expected for the twenty-first century.

Perhaps not surprisingly, the rise of commercialization and the evolution toward private property led to a growing individualism and a matching global culture that began to affect urban Ottoman society. To cite a minor symptom for Ottoman Muslims, the trend toward a global culture manifested itself in the use of first names devoid of specific religious connotation. Instead of Ahmed, Mehmed, and Mustafa, we now increasingly find names such as Behcet, Ra'fet, Rami, Rif'at and Şevket, among others.[127] The shift to less religiously "loaded" first names allowed non-Muslim Ottomans to use some of these neutral Ottomanized names, occasionally as surnames. This use of religiously neutral surnames provides further evidence of the participation and integration of non-Muslim ethnic groups into the common culture of the larger commercialized Ottoman society.[128]

Conclusions

When we shift our approach away from the political structure and focus on society, the specificities of Ottoman transformations in the "middle period" appear in the cultural sphere as well. The symbiotic interethnic relationships so forged are analogous to the ones manifest in Spain under Arab-Muslim rule. Here we encounter Ottoman-Armenian, -Greek, or -Jewish artifacts and products. Ottoman-Armenian and Ottoman-Jewish literary texts have particularly interested Andreas Tietze, who has studied the interface between poetry and Ottoman Jewish music. He has also published studies of Ottoman-Armenian literature.[129] The social symbiosis displayed by these cultural products points to a society that was less segregated than in earlier, feudal times. For some social groups, it now became possible to build bridges that facilitated daily and regular communication and social contact across cultural divides. In the scholarly literature and in Ottoman contemporary sources, the blurring of social and cultural lines has been portrayed repeatedly as symptomatic of decline. This approach in the historiography appears to have some merit as long as one equates the traditional with the "classical"— that is, the enduring norms of the society in question. The perpetual goal of certain elements of Ottoman society is deemed to be adhesion to tradition. While this thesis has been a dominant and guiding one in Ottoman historiography, however, I hold an opposite interpretation, namely, that the cultural bridges of the "middle centuries" show the capacity of the society to adapt to new social and economic conditions.

In most of the recent scholarly discourse on Ottoman society, only one side of the dialogue between cultures is consciously stated. Ottoman culture is almost always described

from the outsider's point of view. By leaving the dialogue between observer and observed on the unconscious level, the
possibilities for comparison and contrast between the two
cultures are lost, and so are the relations established between the investigators and their subject. The reader is left
with the notion that Ottoman culture is unique. If it were
left at that, not much harm would perhaps be done. But by
postulating incommensurability between Ottoman and
European civilizations, recent scholars usually resort to es-
sentialist analyses which are, moreover, nearly always proposed on an ad hoc basis. The social processes and their local
and temporal contexts are usually left out of the picture.
Therefore developments in Ottoman history appear unilinear, and motivations for action and change are visualized as
socially uncontested, clear, and frictionless. In the end,
choices that have been made by social forces are not isolated
and identified. The human agents are always missing. The
analyses, when offered, provide no bases for comparison,
nor do they attempt to give material for any meaningful answers to the question "why?" Perhaps we should query why
our society will allow some of its scholars to operate within
these crippling limitations.

If the very broad outline of social trends presented here
for the Ottoman "middle period" is accurate, it would seem
that the dominant processes of Ottoman history were not
begun in the formative centuries. The importance of the
gazi tradition has perhaps been overestimated, and so have
the developments leading to a nation-state and experiments
with the European version of modernity. The dominant
processes were set in motion in the "middle years," when a
greater number of individuals—members of the commercial
or urban classes—benefited equally from the somewhat
open society of the time. The picture proposed here stands
in direct contrast to certain analyses of the present course
of historical development. I strongly disagree with the view
that the societies of southwestern Asia have no option
but to spend their human and material resources in pursuit
of the goal of the nation-state, fixed vainly on goals of
autarchy.

In this study the emphasis has been placed on society rather than the state. The state was weak in the seventeenth and eighteenth centuries and, at least where certain sectors of society were concerned, seems to have allowed for experiments in tolerance and social diversity. There apparently existed less exclusiveness, differentiation, and segregation along confessional and ethnic lines than has been postulated to date. Yet these differences did not wither away, or else the clamor for nation-states based on ethnic homogeneity would not have been rewarded by the formation of exclusive polities.

Finally, let me end with a word of caution and a disclaimer. The revival of the Ottoman Empire, or any other, is not on the proposed agenda of this study.[130] Rather, by freeing our analyses from the nation-state approach, we can better assess the role of social and cultural symbioses in the early modern period, with an eye to different historical trajectories and a distinctive historical development. This study confronts the distortions of the standard "nationalist" retrospective approach. At a minimum, such an approach allows analysts to judge, wrongly in my opinion, that enmities among the various confessional, ethnic, and linguistic groups are primordial. The clichés we face paint as immemorial ill will between Turks on the one hand, and Greeks, Armenians, and Arabs, let alone South Slavs, on the other. In the daily press examples abound of these enmities from more recent history: Christian versus Muslim, for instance, or Arab versus Israeli.

Once it is established that primordialism is ahistorical (as it is demagogic and racist), it becomes possible to demonstrate that there were times when the various confessional, ethnic, and linguistic groups in Ottoman society interacted in various symbiotic ways, albeit on a limited scale. These interactions suggest a certain openness within Ottoman society to the identity of each constituent group. At the same time it is important to not lose sight of the larger containing structure as it was undergoing transformation. The social experiments that permitted a pluralist society to function are lost in the historical debris, left over in the wake of our attempts to chart the historical trajectory of the culturally homogenizing, unilineal nation-state. It is by retrieving that abandoned historical record that the posssibilities for writing the history of southwest Asian society in the twenty-first century become conceivable. The vision is one of a future society that will thrive on symbiotic coexistence and plurality.

Author's note: Isenbike Togan, by her example, provided inspiration for the conception of this study. At two conferences at Munich and in Strasbourg, parts of this study were delivered as lectures. I am grateful to the sponsors of these two conferences and to several friends who commented on earlier versions of this study. Two of them, namely Talal Asad (New York) and Ramkrishna Mukherjee (Calcutta), and three generations of graduate students participating in my seminar on "Historical Precedents for Multi-Cultural Societies, an Agenda for the Twenty-first Century" (at California State University, Long Beach) have taken the time to give detailed and much appreciated comments. They have saved the writer from many errors of interpretation. Copyediting of this manuscript was done by Marina Preussner and a copy-editor for the *International Journal of Middle East Studies.*

Appendixes

Notes

Bibliography

Index

Appendix A

Sixteenth Century Evidence for Decentralization and Experimentation with Revenue or Income Expropriation

Early examples of both decentralization and experimentation in taxation are suggested by the sources even for the sixteenth century and more frequently in the seventeenth. For the late sixteenth century, we have evidence from 'Ali, who complains that office had been turned into income instead of service. (References are from Andreas Tietze's two volume translation of Ali's *Counsel.*) Among the examples he cites are:

1. A *Beylerbeyi* who acts as his own *defterdar.*
2. Changes in the *ihtisap.*
3. Increase in the use of *iltizam.*
4. A growing number of sons of paşas who get *ziamets* as income.
5. Over zealous use of *nuzul u avariz.*
6. The abuse of *baqaya-i qadime.*
7. Abuse by the monopolists or *muhtekirs* of corn.
8. The use of ziamets and *timars* as pledge for delivery of revenue to treasury (II, 43).
9. *Umal* and *boluk halki* and iltizams (II, 98, n. 98).

Below is a detailed outline from four of these:

1. 'Ali challenges the idea that provincial governors double up by acting as their own defterdars or act as their own treasurers. This is suggestive of their growing autonomy and independence. The governors use the "office" of *eyalet defterdar* as a means of self-enrichment; in Ali's own words: "that the beylerbeyis of the outlying provinces should not be made inspectors of the finances (of their province) and that the royal treasury and the public treasury (beytü l-mal-i muslimin) should not be allowed to be destroyed by their highhanded interferences" (I, 64).

   Ali's point of view reflects that of a defterdar who regrets that beylerbeyis were put in charge of inspecting *vilayet* level finances and used it as a way of enriching themselves. But in fact, the implication is that the governors were acting more and more independently of Istanbul when they saw their office as mainly a means of accumulating income, very much on the order of property.

   'Ali reports from his personal experience as defterdar of Baghdad (in 992/1584), where the competitors for the office of beylerbeyi were bidding money (40,000 gold pieces) for the Baghdad governorship. Then he adds: "Why should they then offer that much gold and should be that eager after the governorship of Baghdad? With this question in mind," 'Ali continues, "I investigated the receipts of one of them. I learned that on account of being the agent (*ma-bayn*) of the finance directors in one year he collected one hundred and ten *yük* of aspers for the imperial treasury and two hundred and forty *yük* aspers for that devastated ruin that was his own treasury" (ibid., I, p. 65).

2. 'Ali also complains about the conversion of offices into iltizam: one consequence to which he objects is social mobility. To him it has special implications for the lower ranks of society; thus he complains that appointments were being made not on the basis of merit but on how much money one can raise to pay for the office; " . . . offices not be given by way of iltizam. . . . " 'Ali

complains about the giving of office in the form of ilt-izam (the view that an office is measured by the revenue which accrues to it, therefore it is viewed simply as an income or revenue producing source, rather than one for which the candidate will need to have special qualifica-tions to serve (the idea of a bureaucracy which required special training or even knowledge is negated here); and especially since this very process is used as an entree into higher offices by men of low ranks (e.g., those who aspire and get position of *çavuş* or that of *müteferriqa*);

'Ali also objects to administrative parcellization of governorships or *beylerbeyliks*. Because of his "pro-sipahi prejudice" 'Ali does not see that this was a means of spreading "rewards" or income as the sources of rev-enue became more and more scarce.

The examples of division of beylerbeyiliks cited by 'Ali are of the provinces of the Yemen and Bosnia: the names of the recipients and the problems encountered are related by 'Ali. He especially cites the case of Gazi Ferhad Bey/Paşa, of the Sokollu family, the governor of Bosnia, who although a cousin of Ali's patron Lala Mus-tafa Paşa, did not seem to get along with 'Ali. At some point having served in the entourage of this said Ferhad, he has some very telling, first-hand observations to make about this individual, and especially calls into question his "orthodoxy" as a Muslim (I, 71–75).

3. changes in the ihtisap or *narkh-i ruzi* (standard prices): Ali's complaint is that if the inspectors or *muhtasibs* were not drawn from knowledgeable and expert ones, then those from the low class might become enriched and the military class would become bankrupt. It has been already pointed out in the body of the study that the ihtisab was viewed in the early sixteenth century as a source of income (see Jerusalem *sicil* reference). The example cited illustrates that the ihtisap was part of the fief income or timar of the *sanack bey* of Jerusalem. Those who became inspectors (muhtasibs) were the ones who could afford to buy the right from the sancak bey. The working of the ihtisap in the first half of the

sixteenth century was a matter settled upon by the kadi, the muhtasib and the *ahl al-suka* or men of the market, that is, either guild members or merchants. Thus, the reaya had no voice in the determination of the standard prices. So again 'Ali shows his "class" bias, as before when he had no sympathy for social or economic or political mobility. Here he repeats this prejudice: "The farm absentees (*renjber, manav*), break out of the circle of poverty, their situation improves, and the rope of their livelihood that was tied to destitution begins to be disentangled by the hand of affluence. Of course, (other) peasants (*ra'iyet tayefesi*) who are their relatives see them and undertake it to abandon agriculture, to settle in cities and towns, and to make a living there. (Consequently) the soldiers of Islam ... on the one hand lose their peasants and on the other hand are forced to procure their daily bread paying manifold increased prices." (ibid.., 25–26)

Then 'Ali alludes to provincial practices of the ihtisap: "The strangest thing in this respect is the bizarre method of standard prices current in the provinces of Egypt, Damascus, and Aleppo, and in general in the flourishing lands of the Arabs. The stock of all the foodstuff of the notables is the protection afforded to one store of each kind.... " Ibid. What 'Ali complains about is the fact that the *ahl- al suqa* seem to bribe those who protect them so that they could violate the ihtisap price list. (This again shows that the reaya had no one to protect them from the corruption of the ihtisap system.) 'Ali complains that at one time when members of the *ilmiye* served as muhtasibs and hence defended the interests of the reaya, the system could not be corrupted. But at no point does he indicate the interests the ulema served, even as he asserts that the ulema as muhtasibs protected the interest of the reaya, this would represent ideal practice rather than reality.

4. Among *kanun* violations, he condemns the awarding of "fiefs" or timars and ziamets to vezirs' followers. One of

his main objections is that the timars and ziamets were viewed by these people as a source of income rather than means for perpetuating the sipahi system. Here again, 'Ali does not see that the whole system of revenue extraction was rapidly changing, and that with the change experienced by the timar system, the fiefs are now treated mainly as fiscal devices, rather than as rewards for service (I, 84–85).

The practice of awarding timars and ziamets to followers of the vezirs, beylerbeyis and *ümera* is unprecedented by former sultanic standards, especially when such award occurs in the lifetime of the superior officer concerned. In the past, at the death of one of these great ones, a few of their followers were so honored, but the rest of their men were assigned to bölüks of Egypt or Baghdad or other border provinces. Not only did assignment of timars to the men of a dignitary constitute an abuse of established practice, it also meant that the grandees would divert the *hass* revenues assigned to them for the equipment and support of their men, to commerce, thus making themselves merchants. As they enrich themselves, deserving candidates for appointment to ziamets and timars wait in vain since there are not enough "fiefs" around to accomodate both the men of the great ones and them. 'Ali reports episodes from his tenure as *timar defterdari* of Aleppo, where he found that some of the beylerbeyis of Aleppo may have had a hass to which accrued one million in revenues, and that the revenue saved by appointing his own retainers to timar and ziamet came to eight hundred thousand aspers. Further, 'Ali complains that during his tenure as timar defterdar no timars were assigned to men who had been out of office as part of their rotation. When one of the holders of a ziamet dies, one of his own men inherits his ziamet improperly. Such practices lead to the disintegration of the old order. Ali's remedy is that the sultan will have to go back to the kanun practices whereby only the deserving are appointed to these incomes. 'Ali views the appointments mainly as bureaucratic practices, that is, to an office rather than to an income, hence his call for return to the imagined or remembered old system (ibid., 85–86).

Appendix B

Koçu Bey harks back to the ideal past which he describes in contrast with the contemporary "reality" which he also described. In the *Risale*, the author who wrote his treatise in 1041/1631–1632, does not draw separately the contrasting characteristics of these two pictures. In the Appendix, I have abstracted and divided the two in order to highlight the contrast. Repetition is a function of Koçu's own presentation. (The *Risale*'s abstractions and outline that are made here were based on my own translation of the Ottoman text, published in Istanbul, 1277/1861. This fresh translation from the Ottoman Turkish was necessitated by the different approach which I am taking to this material from those attempted by others before me. Since the treatise is quite short, twenty-nine pages, and the outline below is quite detailed, I did not feel it necessary to provide page numbers.)

Details of the Ideal Picture from Koçu

    I. Adab al-Saltanah
      The state as it should be:
      A. Sultan shall be at helm, no delegation of authority or mediation by *nudema* or favorites. It

is this system which made the Ottomans and their territories both *mahrusa* and *ma'mura*, safe and prosperous.

1. Favorites, *iç* and *diş halki* (inner and outer service of the sultan's palace) were sent away from court to provincial service.

   Sultan Süleyman in person attended to public affairs at divan, except at the end of his reign.

   The etiquette of his sultanate or *adab al-saltanah* is repeated as the paradigm that should be emulated, thus teaching by example.

B. Vezirs should be given long enough tenure to be effective, for example, grand vezir Sokollu Mehmed; till 982/1574 grand vezirs had complete freedom in appointments and in the conduct of *maslahat* (public affairs) and had direct access to the sultan.

   1. Grand Vezir completely independent; the vezirs knew what they were doing.

   2. *Damads* (imperial son-in-law) were sent out into provinces. . . . They were honest, intelligent men who served well on the frontier. They were assigned to supervise, in trust, *khavas* and *muqata'at*.

   3. Vezirs came from the pool of experienced administrators, those who first were sancak beys or beylerbeys. Then they were assigned first to be beylerbey of Anadolu, then Rumeli, before elevation to the *kubbe alti* (Imperial Council) vezirate.

C. Imperial livings, pensions, shall be given only to *zaims*, and timariots, and of those only the deserving;

D. External signals of distinctions and social lines (of clothing and practices such as public horse-riding and sword bearing), were maintained, and are to remain distinctly drawn: everyone thus knows his function and place (and it will be easy to see from both attire and public demeanor, where each individual stands);

E. *Beylerbeyi* and *sancak bey* appointments shall be given to those qualified:
1. Twenty to thirty year tenure (almost for life).
2. Their military (and civic) duty, rather than personal prosperity, was top priority for them.

II. The Condition of timar holders and zaims (or Ahval-i timar u ziamete)
A. The services rendered by them in past are spelled out: a kind of etiquette or *adab-i sipahiyan* is maintained that specifies who the sipahis were and how they served; in the past they served loyally, and there was no need for *kapi kullari* for the waging of successful campaigns.
1. Gives their numbers.
2. Those assigned to Rumeli to Anadolu defended their respective territories, neither needing the other.
3. No *ecnebis*, or outsiders, were allowed into the ranks of timar holders.
B. "Etiquette" or Adab-i Sipahiyan
There was a certain autonomy exercised by the "corps," especially in the matter of ascertaining who properly belonged to it.

The sipahis were the pillars of the *din u devlet:* maintaining local order and expansion of imperial domains were their main achievements in the past.
1. The earlier campaigns and conquests were carried out successfully thanks to them.
2. Loyal and faithful.
3. No need for *kapi kullari.*
4. *adab*
   a. No ecnebi/outsiders.
   b. *Dirliks* inherited.

    c. They provided their own legitimation and authentication, and were self-policed.

    d. Service with *baş u dil* (body and soul) at campaign required for promotion (none if recepient stays at capital).

    e. Settle at their timar always under their *bayrak* or colors.

    f. Followed military orders when they were assigned to an operation.

    g. Vacant *ziamets* assigned to holders of *eyalet beylerbeylik*.

    h. *Beylerbey* assigns timar or ziamets.

    i. Loyal to din u devlet, religion and state.

III. Tavayif or groups who benefitted from *ulufe* (salary stipend): *Adab-i yeniçeriyan* or etiquette of janissaries: who were the *yeniçeris*, and what was their order?

In the year 982 A. H. during the reign of Murad III, there were 36,153 men listed as yeniçeris distributed amongst twenty-nine *tavayif/cema'at*.

A. Prescribed *vezayif* or livings came from treasury.

B. Numbers could be increased or decreased.

C. Kept distinct from the sipahis, esp. when it came to livings: sipahis had their timars, and so forth.

D. Etiquette or adab-i yeniçeriyan spelled out:

    1. Sources of recruitment.

    2. Settlement triangle in cities of Istanbul-Bursa-Edirne.

    3. *Devşirme* spelled out (i.e., what it is as a practice).

    4. Prescription for graduation.

    5. Settle in barracks, as bachelors.

    6. Those who were tardy in reporting for campaign service were struck off *ulufe*, in perpetuity.

    7. Conditions for retirement spelled out.

    8. No dismissal without cause, served specified terms.

9. Punishment by peers (*agas* in *divan*), but children of the guilty culprit were given timar or ziamet.

IV. Status of the *kanun* of the *ilmiye* (judicial/scholarly career) and its changes: (*adab-i tarikat ilmiye* and its deterioration into *mahsubiye* = favoritism).

After declaring that *şar'* and *din* (Holy Law and religion) when upheld, had brought the great favors enjoyed by the Ottoman dynasty, Koçu indicates that the *rasm* (path, true road) for the ulema was: merit, experience, and wisdom. That is what counted when decisions on appointments had to be made. *Muftis, kazaskers,* and so forth, were not dismissed: for example, Ebu-s Su'ud served for life and was honored for life; those who chose retirement did so voluntarily and were given a specific retirement and pension. As a result, good services were rendered, and also many a pious and socially useful endowment was established. (Changes, according to Koçu Bey, noted below)

V. Changes in the *ulufeli tavayif* (or salaried troops): Koçu notes the difference in the number of *ulufeli kul taifesi.*

   A. They used to number ninety-two, two hundred six.

   B. Lived in triangle: Edirne, Istanbul, Bursa.

VI. In explanation of the conditions of the *reaya* (subjects, commons, mainly peasants) *Risale* pp. 16–17). (This is one of the shorter sections of Koçu's *Risale.* This limited treatment lends further evidence to the contention that in fact the writers of this genre were least concerned with the reaya, and then primarily as generator of revenue.)

   A. Up to the year 990 the taxes levied were:

      1. Forty to fifty akçe *cizye* per head.

      2. Forty akçe as *avariz.*

      3. One akçe per two head of sheep as adet-i agnam (sheep tax).

B. The mübaşirlar (collectors) got their "fee," two to five (akçe) each for *avariz* and *ghulamiye/ghilamiye.*

C. Income from the *khavass* = 2,441 yük akçe (2,44,100,000) (in contrast to the revenue generated in Koçu's period: only 100 yük = 100,000, were collected).

Conditions Prevailing in Koçu's Time

The specifics of evidence for the the dissolution of the old orders is illustrated by Koçu through his analysis of changes:

I. In the status of the timars and ziamets, these are listed as:

A. Sipahis lost an autonomy once exercized by the "corps," especially in way of ascertaining who belonged to the sipahis.

B. Bases for awarding the ziamet and timar changes. They are no longer awarded in the old manner, but rather as favors, or through bribery, and so on.

C. The beneficieries of these changes were the *vükela* of the governors and vezirs and their kapi halki, that is, the men of their households, which were composed of their own slaves and entourage.

D. The original system of ziamets and timars has disappeared completely, and the sipahi way of life is finished! Those who receive appointments are the lackies of vükela, rather than virtuous hereditary members of the sipahi class. Thus, the system was no longer regarded mainly as one which produced sipahis, as illustrated by the example above and the fact that even reaya and city dwellers can enter the corp through *intisap* (influence and nepotism), bribery, or purchase. (Koçu Bey bewails the treatment of office as sources of income rather than the service which the assignment of source of income was supposed to be exchanged for. Put simply, it will not be long before these are bought and sold as commodities by merchants and financiers.)

The basis for the way the ziamets and timars were held was changing, and this had to be recognized. What are the new bases?

1. Koçu notes that the change in feudal land signified transformation of a system of reward for service into a form of pure payment as intisap became the primary means of obtaining a holding.

   The critical date for the change is the year 992/1584. The timar and ziamet villages and farms were gradually given to the followers of great men of state. They became the ma'kal = livelihood/livings of the great, who turned these into dirliks (stipends), *taka'ud* (retirement benefices), *hass, vakif,* and even acquired them as temlik = private property. Hence most of the claims on the ziamets and timars are disputed, or *niza'lu.*

   One of the secondary steps in this process of conversion of ziamets and timars into outright sources of income was to hold them as *sepet* (unassigned, in order to divert this source of income for other uses).

   With the introduction of the *kapi kullari* as police in the provinces and country, the sipahis' original functions of maintaining law and order in the provinces and participate in campaigns were curtailed.

   That the new holders of the timars and ziamets (during Koçu Bey's lifetime) saw their function as other than military is evidenced by their high expenditures on the display of silver ornaments and decorations in

dress and equipment, but neglect of the ostensible military functions of their "office."

II. Orders or *tavayif* who benefitted from salaries (ulufe): in the year 982/1574, in the reign of Murad III,
there were 36,153 men among the yeniçeris distributed amongst twenty-nine tavayif/cema'at.

   A. As of 991/1583 ecnebis entered corp and during
   the circumcision feast, ("sur") as a one time
   exception a crowd admitted into corp with the
   intercession of the *nudema* (sultan's boon companions); also ferzand-i sipahi (the sons of sipahis) were invited to gain entrance into the corps.

   B. In 1030/1620–1621 another innovation (called
   becayeş) made it possible and common for
   "outsiders," including sons enter by buying a
   place in the corp.

   C. *Oturak* (garrison duty) extended to 10,000 individuals.

   D. Campaigns drew 200,000 men of indescribable
   backgrounds.

   E. Ulufes were sold by those who held them.

   F. The nominal janissaries located everywhere,
   they had taken over regions and areas as their
   possessions; beys, kadis, and muhasil-i emval
   (tax collectors) were paralyzed in their duties.

   G. During campaigns only 7,000–8,000 would
   show up.

   H. Under these circumstances how could society
   be ordered?

      1. Prescribed vezayif came from any source of
      income, not only the treasury.

      2. Numbers increased at will.

      3. They were assigned livings from sources set
      aside for the support of sipahis, and thus be-
      came confused with the latter. In other words,
      their stipends came from all over, including
      assignments of timars, khass, and so forth.

      4. Etiquette of the janisarries (adab-i yeniç-
      eriyan) violated by:

a) Changes in the sources of their recruitment.

b) Settlement outside the triangle of cities: (Istanbul-Bursa-Edirne).

c) Violation of the *devşirme* system.

d) Violation of prescription for "graduation."

e) Those settled in the barracks were no longer used exclusively for bachelors.

f) Retention of salaries by those tardy in campaign.

g) Changes in their janissary retirement procedure.

h) Dismissal without cause, short of their regular service terms.

i) Loss of corporate autonomy symbolized by punishment by peers.

III. Changes in the kanun of the ilmiye (learned men): since 1003 A.H., the ilmiye recruitment procedures and corps constitution changed beyond recognition: *fevk al-hadd*. Kanun disregarded.

A. Ulema subjected to dismissal without cause, and the occupants of high office have no access to the sultan: vükela hold fate of ilmiye in their hands.

B. Appointments to high office are without meaning, being made through intisap rather than through *ilm* (learning), and therefore the path of attaining ilmiye status was "transformed!"

C. Ulema fall prey to the temptations to display luxurious households and large retinues.

D. *Mülazamets* (candidacy for ilmiye office) sold by the ulema (to those who could pay). (What Koçu Bey bewails is the turning of posts even in the religious establishment into income-producing propositions and that therefore, those who had the money, and not necessarily the merit, could enter the corp); Koçu Bey's remedy: no more mülazamets until posts filled and no waiting list exists.

E. Kadis also lose prestige and respect also because any *subaşi* (meaning minor official)
could successfully challenge their authority.
There was no *hürmet* (reverence, respect)
left for them.

IV. Changes in the ulufeli tavayif (or boluk tayife):
Koçu Bey notes the difference in the number of ulufeli kul taifesi from the earlier times when they
were lean. They used to be 92,206 and lived in triangle cities Edirne, Istanbul, Bursa.

A. Became 200,000 (and he then wonders how the
latter were to be provided for and financed!).

B. Until year 992/1584, they were "clean" and
amenable to command, then a change took
place in recruitment patterns.

V. In explanation of the conditions of the reaya *Risale*
(pp. 16–17).

A. After 990/1582:

1. To accommodate increased expeditures for
salaries due to rise in the number of those
enrolled in the corps:

a) Forty to fifty akçe to two hundred forty
akçe as *cizye* per head.

b) Three hundred akçe per *hane* as avariz.

c) One akçe per *koyun* as *resm-i agnam*.

2. Also there were conversions of the *khavas*
into temlik, vakif and *paşmaklik*.

The Sultan must attend to these: (by) "seeing to
the regularization of the status of affairs of the
fukara' people, is one of heaven's requirements
from emperors!"

VI. Why there is spread of insurrection (fasad) and up-
heaval (fitneh) and loss of domains to enemy: (pp.
20–21) There are so many campaigns against the
enemies of the faith (*a'day-i din*) this had led to un-
told loss of property and treasure (*mal u khaza'in*).
This, in turn, is due to the losses of Muslim domains to the enemies.

Some of the reasons for such losses:

A. Since 990/1582, posts have been assigned in return for bribes (ruşvet) to those who were not qualified (na-ehilne).

B. From 1004/1595–1596, celalis are rampant in Anadolu.

C. Since 1005/1596–1597, thirty provinces have been lost, including eastern provinces lost to the Safavi Şah, Yemen, and so forth.

(Again, Koçu Bey does return in the treatise, to the theme of giving "officers" independence for the duration of their tenure in office [in some instance perpetual or unlimited, or even limited], but with a specified period, for example, seven years as in this case under discussion).

Given the assumption of writers like Koçu Bey, that the office is an objective, fixed entity, with defined functions, procedures and rules (hence the adab dimension of the discussion of these commentators), it is quite inconceivable to them (they claim) to fathom the view that office meant income or a source of income, hence an investment. At least, this is the view they seem to be bemoaning. But in reality, office was income not only in the time of a Koçu Bey, but also in that of 'Ali, who makes the same complaint, even probably in the classical period. As we have indicated elsewhere, these authors were projecting an idealized picture onto the past, a picture that in fact had never existed in reality.

Appendix C

Feyzullah Efendi, the Şeyhülislam, had authorized the issuing of the following instructions to the several provinces of the Sultan, ostensibly to rectify certain deviations from religious practices, due to negligence and laxity on the part of both the local populations and the ilmiye officials assigned to guide their moral and religious instruction. Although coached in the form of religious reform, the subtext of the following documents reveals an attempt on the part of the sultan's chief advisor to bolster the ruler's eroding political support by requiring obedience to the sultan's authority.

To the Great Mollas, Kadis and Muftis of Hodavandigar Sanjak, order that: "Religion is right counsel!" (al-dinul-nasihah = The true faith is proper admonition). In conformity with the correctness of this sacred hadith, for the general well-being of all Muslims of all the classes (tabaqat) who fall under the shadow of the sultanate's wings and live in a state of repose and comfort in the domains far and wide; and wishing to take as model and to conform to the sacred text: "And let there be (formed) of you an *ummah* (whose members) seek the good, act righteously and forbid evil-doing, verily those are the very ones who are prosperous!"

First. You are to test and examine the imams (those who lead the prayers) and the *khatibs* (the hutba sayers, that is, the preachers) everywhere; you are to confirm in their places those (of them) who are of the Sunni faith, experts in both the recitation of the Glorious Quran and the matters of prayers; and in the process, those among them who show a defect or a lack of qualification should be required to prepare (and qualify) and make up (the lack); once this has been done, you are to communicate to the Sublime Threshold the appointments and petitions of those who meet these three qualifications, and (therefore are) deserving (of being) appointed (to these posts as imams and khatibs).

Second. The noble precepters (*muddersin-i kiram*) who (normally) teach and instruct in the various sciences and the several arts in the medreses and halls (of learning *mahafel*, i.e., circles) which had been donated for God's grace (as pious acts), for benefit, they are to come forward and teach on the appointed (and regular) days, they are to stick to each lesson in the books of *tafsir, hadith* and *fiqh* which are the arenas of eternal felicity and the means to righteous acts; and in this above manner constantly, they are to function and they are to resist completely from not so acting so that: these sciences which are the heritage of the prophets, this (following) hadith (*sa'adet nemunda mübayen ve mazbut*) which by way of graduation they know its importance, it is clearly and correctly shown: " 'Ilm/Science is three (parts): strong faith, upheld sunna, and just ordinance. Everything else is considered extra or excess good deed; and those of this group (of teachers) who in accordance with the order (given) are either tardy in following the order or are incapable or ignorant, they are also to be reported, out of piety (or in words of order: "livechi llah, la gharadh siwah" = for God, of whom there is no other purpose)".

Third. Inspect the preachers and repetiteurs (vu'az ve muzakirin), to a certain that in the use of their position they teach canon law (problems), religious tasks and good conduct, and that they soften and rarify the hearts of the believers through the use of the well-regarded (standard =) *mu'tabarah* books; they are to avoid the adorned false tales ... lest in their relation they mislead the innocents, or lest through fanaticism and call for prejudice, they lead to creating dissentions and hatreds and the sparkling of a rejoicing at others' misfortunes. However, by conveying through the use of well-regarded books and well-founded problems, they, by being wary of being blamed as imams, should not leave out the admonition of doing the right thing and forbidding the resort to what is undesirable (hathar ile amr ma'ruf wa nahi 'an al-munkar terk etmeyip; in accordance with: "verily when Allah had made agreement with those to whom the Book was delivered, in order that they should explain it to the people, and not to keep it secret ... ," strive and exert themselves to act to inform according to the canonical rules (ahkam) and presciptions of repetition (sharayet-i tezkir), and to expose in instruction of ethics (adab) and preaching (va'z) the (work) of the great jurists; and also of this group those who are not deserving (and continue in office) are to be reported (as in the earlier manner).

Fourth. Look into the *mektebs* (schools for children); those who teach boys (teenagers) and precept youths, those who are pure and pious and capable of recitation of the Koran, and those of the teachers who are capable of giving exegesis, who communicate and teach the beliefs of followers of the Sunnah and Consensus (ahlu alsunna waljama'ah) from the traditional Arabic and Turkish treatises, these are to be confirmed in their posts; and those who are not capable are to be replaced by those who are.

Fifth. The commonality of Muslims and the totality of the monotheists are to be made to strive and acquire knowledge of conditions which are related to prayers, fasting, pilgrimage, the tithe, and other problems pertaining to belief and practice and the requirements of the faith; and to adhere fully as should be to the Friday and communal prayers and while their children are occupied with learning the Koran and engaged in understanding the perquisites of the faith and striving, they are to beware of preoccupation with worldly deceptions; and in the exercise of paternal rights of discipline they are to strive hard and exert themselves to the full; and village inhabitants and those who live in woolen tents (nomads), also, in the fore-outlined manner, are also to learn and attain the requisites of Islam. In order that they might do so and keep the five prayers and the communal prayer, one of the *medrese*-students is to be assigned to reside amongst them, and to warn and insist upon the rennovation and maintenance of the mosques and mektebs (schools). In the towns and the villages the centers of learning and reading and places of prayer and worship are not to be in disuse; in order for them to be kept habitable and livable, you are to exert your utmost and insist on that, so much so that this desireable quality would attract the blessing of the Blesser, and requirements of security and traquility and the (admonition?) is hereby clearly attested to by the sacred hadith, "kama takunu yuwalla 'alaykum" (As You Are So Shall Ye Be Ruled).

And thou who art authorized to give *fetvas*, the aformentioned mollas, this matter whose fulfilment is required, in completing it (by cooperating) in conformity to the divine order "Join Hands In Doing Good Deeds And Piety," are to be as one with the kadis (hukam-i şer') of the districts (kazas); show religious zeal in the performance of the rites of loyalty and ... facilitation of the values and requirements of the Religious Law.

In accordance with the letter of the incumbent Seyhulislam Feyzullah, a ferman has been issued requiring its execution and authorization.

When this ferman, which has been issued in this matter, and the letter of the said molla has arrived, they are to be acted upon, and furthermore, under whosoever supervsion in the kaza-capital this letter arrives, it is to be entered into the court records and you are to execute and act upon its illustrious contents.

(Dated Beginning of Zilhijjeh, 113/ April/May, 1702.)

Copies to Kadis and Muftis at: Sultan Onu, Karasi, Bolu.

Copies to Kadis and Muftis at: Baghdad, Basra, Mosul, Sehrizor.

(Those last four dated 20 Safar, 1114/ July 17, 1702.)

Copies to Kadis and Muftis at sancaks and districts of: (1) Vize, (2) Cirmen, (3) Kirk Kilise, (4) Selanik, (5) Tirhala, (6) Rumeli sagh kolu, (7) Rumeli orta kolu and (8) Rumeli sol kolu, (9) Anadolu Eyalet, (10) Sivas Eyalet, (11) Karaman Eyalet, (12) Adana Eyalet, (13) Sam Eyalet, (14) Trablus Sam Eyalet, (15) Safad-Sayda Beirut, (16) Halep Eyalet, (17) Rakka Eyalet, (18) Marash Eyalet, (19) Diyarbekir Eyalet, (14) Erzurum Eyalet, (15) Trabzon Eyalet, (16) Kars Eyalet, (17) Çildir Eyalet, (18) Van Eyalet, (19) Timişvar's Muhafiz, Molla and Mufti and, (20) Belgrade's Muhafiz, Molla and Mufti. From Mühimme defteri 112, 191–193.

Hukm to the Vali of Bosna, Molla of Bosna Sarayi, and the Kadis of Bosna Eyalet: Because it has come to our Imperial hearing that in the towns and villages of the great lands which are the center of the ulema of the faith and the collectivity of the jurisprudents of the Muslims, there are Muslims who are residents and inhabitants who have set aside, ignored and are not preoccupied with the learning of *ilm-i hal* and from the benefits of religious affairs, the exaltation of the acceptable canons and (since verily) the understanding of the various precepts are among the oldest of the responsibilities of the religion and state, and are the most important preoccupations of dominion and community; especially the admonition to act righteously and forbid evil-doing, for in accordance to the true statement:

"And let there be (formed) of you an ummah (whose members) seek the good, act righteously and forbid evil-doing, verily those are the very ones who are prosperous!" Being of the responsibilities of the faith which are the path to success and the path to triumph and good deeds, (and) abandoning and leaving it, Allah forbid!, would lead to decline of religious observance, the faith and the spread of (darkness) ignorance, loss of direction, and the ruin of the lands, and the perishing of the people, (other than leading to these above disasters), and guided by: "And they had not desisted from evil-doing

which they had committed, may what they were doing end in disaster," being the ugliest of reminders.
In the towns and villages located in Bosna Eyaleti
the Muslim (inhabitants) have displayed illiteracy
and ignorance in the requirements of fasting,
prayer, the hac, and the tithe among the sciences (of
religion). In order to solve these problems, to urge
and ameliorate them to the path of righteousness
through words and deeds, for the revival of the *sunnet* and the explication of the requirements of the
faith and the law, and in order to rectify matters of
this life and the hereafter, one of the ulema, Seyh
Muhammed is being sent to that area with three of
his colleagues.

You, the said vezir, as soon as they arrive in Saray,
you are to secure for them a place to stay in, and
secure for them the assignment of their food and
drink, thereafter should he or one of his companions be sent to areas far or near, they are to be assigned a reasonable number of men. In this matter,
you, being guided by the truthful saying, "Verily
thou shalt cooperate in matters of good deeds and
piety," you are to exert your utmost,; And you the
kadis, also: of the Muslims who are under your
jursdictions in the *kazas*, those of them who are il-
lterate and ignorant, you are to teach them religious
learning in a manner which is suitable. Thus they
will come to understand religious matters, and this
will facilitate the path to good fortune, "In the wish
to please Allah," This is to be done according to:
"and of the people of the book an people or *ummah*
which is constantly reciting Allah's verses during
the night while they prostrate themselves (in
prayers), believing in Allah and the day of judge-
ment, and encouraging acts of righteousness and
discouraging acts of evil-doing, and hasten in the
performance of pious acts, verily these are the very
ones who are good!" You are to help and be parti-
sans of the said molla and his companions in their

call for righteous acts and discouraging evil-doing, thus becoming members of the righteous. Dated Beg. Shevval, 1113.

(Mühimme defteri 112, n.d.) The grand vezir's ferman and imperial signature were added on top of the hukm (to the following effect): "You are to act in accordance with the ferman, which is dubbed mandatory to implement; for the exhaltation of the self evident şer' and celebration of the sublime sunnet of the pride of the Messengers, you are to concentrate your attention, saying, an imperial rescript has been issued.

Appendix D

Shihabudin Al-Khafaji al-Misri al-Hanafi. Outline of his biography. (From Şeyhi, "Vakayiul-fuzela," vol. 1, 140a–b.)

Ahmed b. Mehmed b. Omer famed as Sihabudin Al-Hafaji al-Misri al-Hanafi:

He was born in Cairo, and grew up there. He was under his father's care and education until he arrived at the age of discrimination; thereafter, he studied with his maternal uncle, one of the ulema of Egypt, Ebu Bekir, on whose hands he studied the introduction to the sciences and of Arabic. The remaining arts he studied with the following Arab teachers: Şeyh Mehmed Ramli, Kadi Zakariya, Şaykh Nuruddin Azyadi, Şaykh Ibrahim al-Qami, Şaykh 'Ali b. Ghanem al-Maqdisi, Şaykh Ahmed al'Alqami, and Şaykh Mehmed al-Salihi al-Shami.

He accompanied his father to the hac, and there (in the Hijaz) he settled and frequented the learned circles of such luminaries as 'Ali b. Jarallah, and his grandson Issam. Thereafter, he returned with his father to Egypt. He then travelled to Istanbul, and there studied with the ulema of Rum, especially the Sadr Azmizade Mustafa Efendi on whose hands he acquired the rest of the (ulum) sciences, and then studies with Ganizade Naziri Mehmed Efendi. He then served Murad Han, the second Sa'dudin (Sa'dudinzade Haci Mehmed As'ad Efendi), a thereafter earned the

121

mevleviyet. As usual he then entered the line of schools, and when he was removed from Kirk Akçe medrese, he was awarded some positions in Rum.

1. 1031. Assigned at Siruz Kaza in place of Rodosizade Mustafa Efendi;
2. ——— after his removal, he was assigned to Rhodes Island.
3. ——— after removal assigned to Kamlunce kaza.
4. 1045, Zulkide, having been in the entourage of kapudan Mustafa Paşa, and through his intercession, was assigned Selanik Kaza in place of Yavuzzade S. Mustafa Efendi.
5. 1059. Şevval, removed and his place assigned to Kudsizade Şeyh Mehmed Efendi.
6. 1051. Muherrem, assigned at his birthplace, Cairo, in place of Hocazade 'Ali Efendi.
7. 1051. Zulkide, removed, and in his place Hanafi Mehmed was assigned; he returned to Istanbul.
8. 1052. Jumadi I, upon arriving from Egypt and on not being assigned to the Şeyhulislamate, due to his being accused of openly criticising (the şeyhulislam), as punishment he was exiled to Cairo (Egypt) with the Khanqah kaza (in Egypt) as *arpalik;* thereafter, he was assigned the rank of Istanbul, then that of Anadolu, with that he was given Giza kaza instead of the Khanqah.
9. 1069. Ramazan 12, a Tuesday, he passed away.

While he was famous as a great author and literature, in the matter of *hukumet* or governing a kaza, he was full of injustice and harshness.

The Arabic sources tend to give, in a very summery fashion, the career of this *alim* outside of Egypt. There is a biography compiled by the editor of Ahmad b. Muhammad b. Omar Khafaji, *Rihanet al-'ahiba',* 2 vols. Cairo, 1967. However, the biography is confined to the literary accomplishments of this member of the *ilmiye,* with little information on his appointments outside Egypt.

As a demonstration that the Ottoman chroniclers can provide valuable biographical data on a provincial alim who sought his fortune at the capital, the following is an example. Naima's reports on the occasion for the exile of Khafaji to Egypt, and at the same time demonstrates this alim's daring and defiant attitude even to his patron, the grand vezir. (Reported in the year 1052):

The one famed as Şihab Efendi who after having been given the mevleviyet or as kadi in Egypt, due to his inability to contain his bad temper, and with complaints lodged against him, within seven months of his appointment he was removed and the post was given to Hanafi Efendi. When Şihab Efendi arrived in Istanbul, he started maligning the Şeyhulislam (Zakariyazade Yahya Efendi: 1043–1053/1634–1643 under Murad IV). He (was muntasib to) had *intisap* with the grand vezir (Kemankeş Kara Mustafa Paşa), but because he did not know the language of the day (contemporary scene?), being too daring and *mutasalib* (stubborn, persistent), the grand vezir suffered.

After he was warned to hold his tongue he would not listen (desist). Because he was not awarded (attained) the (office of) şeyhülislam, he very openly critized and cursed the incumbent. For fear that the office of *fetva*, that is, şeyhülislam, might be demeaned and ridiculed, a *ferman* was issued for his (Şihab Efendi) exile. He was put on a *kayak* and sent to the island of Sakiz. The grand vezir, taking pitty on him, had sent patent of the Sakiz kaza (for his upkeep). Because the island was infected with the plague, after a few days' stay, Şihab Efendi, with the excuse that he was escaping the plague, took a *gemi* (back) without permission and arrived in Istanbul. Once he arrived, Şihab Efendi had his clothes changed and appeared before the grand vezir's.

"What is the cause (or meaning) of your having come here without permission?" he was asked.

"My Lord or Ya sultanim, we came to avoid (the infection of) the plague," he answered.

The said *fadil* (the grand vezir) was not pleased by such crudeness of nature (*mertebe-i ghalzet-i tab'*), daring and such belittling of the position of power (i.e., grand vezir's office and person). Out of consideration for the feelings and sensivity of the şeyhülislam, Şihab Efendi was immediately placed on a kayak (which took him) to *Kalib al-Bahr* fort (in the Bogaz) on his way to exile in Egypt."

(Naima editorializes with the conclusion:) "Holding ones tongue, and good behavior of the wise ones, is an important and necessary capital, by all means" Naima, *Tarih*, IV, pp. 17–18.

Notes

1. Compare E. H. Carr, *What is History?* New York: Alfred A. Knopf, 1972, pp. 36–69.

I have addressed some of the historiographical and methodological issues raised here in reviews of significant scholarly monographs in the field of Ottoman and Middle Eastern history. See Rifa'at Ali Abou-El-Haj, "Stanford J. Shaw, *The Ottoman Empire,* vol. 1," *American Historical Review* 82.4 (1977), 1029a-b; "Review of Thomas Naff and Roger Owen eds., *Studies in Eighteenth Century Islamic History*" *The Historian* XLI.4 (1979), pp. 790–91; Amnon Cohen and Bernard Lewis, *Population and Revenue in the Towns of Palestine in the Sixteenth Century,*" *The Muslim World* 78, (1980), pp. 156–58; "Review of V. Volkan and Norman Itzkowitz, *Atatürk,*" *International Journal of Turkish Studies* 4.1 (1987), 149–51; "Review Article: I. Metin Kunt, *The Sultan's Servants*: The Transformation of Ottoman Provincial Government 1550–1650," *Osmanli Araştirmalari* 6 (1986), 221–46.

In papers presented at the Middle East Studies Association meeting, Toronto, 1989, "The Late Ottoman State and the Discourse over Citizens' Rights and (Ottoman) Turkish National Identity During the Two Constitutional Periods," and at a conference on "The State, Decentralization and Tax Farming (1500–1850), The Ottoman Empire, India and Iran," Munich, Spring, 1990, "Efficient Considerations For Theorizing Beyond the Nation-State: The Case of Early Modern and Modern Ottoman Society," I took up the issue of amnesia, which two American scholars, Robert Devereux (*The First Ottoman Constitutional*

Period [Baltimore: Johns Hopkins University Press, 1963]) and Roderic Davison (*Reform in the Ottoman Empire 1856–1876* [Princeton: Princeton University Press, 1963]) displayed in their treatment of the Ottoman constitutional and reform movements in the second half of the nineteenth century. Both authors focused on the inability of Ottoman society to accommodate the liberal traditions contained in the newly adopted Western-style constitution, especially with reference to extending equal rights to non-Muslims. Neither authors found it appropriate to compare the Ottoman experience with the problems American society was facing at the time and for which it fought a civil war. Devereux and Davison published their first monographs in the 1960s—approximately one hundred years after the beginning of the American Civil War—when the question of civil rights for the same African-American minority seemed still to be pending.

Among other problems related to the question of comparative history, I intend to address the phenomenon of amnesia in scholarship on the Middle Eastern and Ottoman studies in some detail in a separate study, "Methods, Methodology, and Historiography in Ottoman and Middle East Studies since *Orientalism.*" There I will discuss other major epistemological issues raised by the scholarship produced, notably in the United States and Western Europe (including United Kingdom), since Edward Said's publication, and comparable scholarship published in the Arab world. The postulate guiding this forthcoming study is the virtual absence of scholarship informed by modern theoretical considerations in history and social science. What is comparative and normative in Ottoman history is rarely the focus of these studies. Ottoman society is not viewed as a human society, subject to change and transformation due to a mixture of its own internal dynamic forces, and sometimes tempered by external ones. Instead, there is continuing theorizing by individual scholars—mostly unconscious, sometimes subjective, but predominantly aberrant—who write with a neo-Orientalist approach confounded by an overly formulaic understanding of theory. At its best the resulting studies are either unidimensional or even fictional in their reconstruction of Ottoman and Middle Eastern society. In notes that follow, I will pick up selected issues resulting from such an approach as I touch upon scholarly trends prevalent in the 1980s.

Halil Berktay is currently engaged in a critical evaluation of the most recent scholarly studies in Turkey on the early Ottoman period. In his paper, "Centralization and Decentralization in the State-Fetichist Perspective of Twentieth Century Turkish Historiography," conference on comparative Ottoman, Safavi, and Mogul histories, (Munich, Germany, Spring, 1990) he evaluated the scholarship of Halil Inalcik and Omer Lütfi Barkan. One of Berktay's main contributions is in the historical context he reconstructed for the kind of approach these two scholars bring to bear on the formative centuries of Ottoman history. The author ties the scholarship produced to the political discourses prevalent in Turkey during the inter-war period.

2. Perry Anderson, *Lineages of the Absolutist State*. London: NLB, 1974. For his reconstruction of Ottoman history, he depends on: H. A. R. Gibb and Harold Bowen, *Islamic Society and the West*, vol. 1, part 1 (London, 1950); Halil Inalcik, *The Ottoman Empire* (London, 1973) and several articles by the same author; Bernard Lewis, *The Emergence of Modern Turkey* (London, 1969). In reading Gibb and Bowen, Anderson relies on criticism by Norman Itzkowitz, "Eighteenth Century Ottoman Realities," *Studia Islamica* 16, (1962). He nevertheless eschews that by Roger Owen, "The Middle East in the Eighteenth Century—On Islamic Decline: A critique of Gibb and Bowen's *Islamic Society and the West*," *Review of Middle East Studies* 1 (1975), pp. 101–12. Owen takes a socioeconomic and sociohistorical approach, while Itzkowitz tends to be institutional. All of the authors on whom Anderson depends subscribe to the notion of rise and decline, and postulate that in the middle period Ottoman society was mostly static, awaiting rejuvenation by modernization as modeled in the West. Huri Islamoglu-Inan evaluates Anderson from other angles (in *The Ottoman Empire and the World-Economy*, Cambridge: Cambridge University Press [1987] p. 385, n. 13,) especially his focus on cultural explanations for the failure of Ottoman society to change, and attributes Anderson's picture of a static society to Orientalist and modernization theories.

3. Anderson's distortion is reminiscent of the treatment of Ottoman history and culture by modern Arab historians. Elsewhere I have noted the use of this distortion as an intellectual foil against which to test a "new history" supporting a modern nation-state ideology for the Arab successor states of the Ottoman empire. See Rifa'at Ali Abou-El-Haj, "The Social Uses for the Past: Recent Arab Historiography of Ottoman Rule," *International Journal of Middle East Studies* 14.2 (1982), 185–201

(French translation appeared simultaneously in *Maghreb Mach-rek* 97 (1982). See n. 76, below, for further evaluation of Anderson's treatment of the concept of the Asiatic Mode of Production and how the AMP further emphasizes the Ottoman different-ness. The most salient feature in Anderson's approach, and one that reflects the secondary sources he consulted, is the percep-tion of Ottoman society as pursuing a unique historical path. In-stead of looking for the normative features that would allow for comparison and contrast with other societies, Anderson sup-presses them in favor of historical evidence for differentness of Ottoman society, indeed "alienness."

4. Anderson, *Lineages*, p. 397. Anderson goes on to say that even contemporary Europeans such as Machiavelli contrasted their social formations, institutions, and governmental systems with those of the Ottomans. In and of itself, this fact does not prove that the observations in question are either objective or scientifically valid. Instead of accepting the statements of Ma-chiavelli and others at face value, we would do better to analyze why European authors of the fifteenth century and later periods felt the need to define themselves as "different." Similarly, the fact that the Ottomans saw themselves as separate from the un-believers does not change the epistemological problem. In both cases, we need to raise the same questions and try to establish the social uses of the ideological labels assigned by authors like Machiavelli and his Ottoman counterparts.

5. Ibid., p. 379.

6. Ibid., pp. 382–83.

7. Halil Inalcik also insists on the impossibility of compar-ing the Ottoman *çiftlik* and European feudalism; see Halil Inal-cik, "Impact of the *Annales* School on Ottoman Studies and New Findings," *Review* (*Journal of the Fernand Braudel Center*, State University of New York, Binghamton, N.Y.) 1:3/4 (1978), 69–96. For a similar emphasis in the European context see Henri Lefebvre, "Marxism Exploded," *Review* 4:1 (1980), 19–32.

8. Compare Lawrence Stone, *The Causes of the English Rev-olution 1526–1642*. London: Routlege and Kegan Paul, 1972.

9. For other contributions to the debate see Boris Porchnev, *Les Soulevements populaires en France au XVIIe siecle*, Paris: Flammarion, 1972; Roland Mousnier, *Peasant Uprisings in Sev-*

enteenth Century France, Russia, and China, London: George Allen and Unwin Ltd., 1971; Emmanuel Le Roy Ladurie, "Les Masses profondes: La paysannerie," in *Histoire economique et social de la France*, vol. 2, *Paysannerie et croissance*, eds. E. Le Roy Ladurie and Michel Morineau, Paris: PUF, 1977, pp. 483–872; Charles Tilly, "War and Peasant Rebellion in Seventeenth Century France," in Charles Tilly, *As Sociology meets History*, New York, London: Academic Press, 1984, pp. 109–44.

10. See Robert Brenner, "Agrarian Class Structure and Economic Development in Pre-Industrial Europe," and idem, "Reply," in *The Brenner Debate*, eds. T. H. Aston and C. H. E. Philpin, Cambridge: Cambridge University Press, 1985. Islamoglu-Inan comments on Brenner's approach and the problem it poses for the understanding of Ottoman society in "State and Peasants in the Ottoman Empire: A Study of Peasant Economy in North-Central Anatolia during the Sixteenth Century," *The Ottoman Empire and the World-Economy*, pp. 105–6, and 404, nn. 1 and 2.

11. For an outline of the debate in European history see Anderson, *Lineages*; T. H. Aston, ed., *Essays from Past and Present: Crisis in Europe 1560–1660*, London: Routledge and Kegan Paul, 1965; Geoffrey Parker and Lesley M. Smith, eds. *The General Crisis of the Seventeenth Century*, London: Routledge and Kegan Paul, 1978; Mousnier, *Peasant Uprisings in Seventeenth Century France, Russia, and China.*

12. See, for example, Jacob van Klaveren, "Fiscalism, Mercantilism and Corruption," in *Revisions in Mercantalism*, ed. D. C. Coleman, London: Methuen, 1969, pp. 140–62.

13. Historians writing in the last decade of the twentieth century find themselves before a major epistemological dilemma. On the global level, most early modern and modern historiography has been guided by the concept of the nation-state as the final goal of the historical process. There looms on the horizon, specifically by 1992, the prospect of the dissolution of the nation-state as we have known it, right at the origin of the creation of the concept in Western and Central Europe. In anticipation of the epistemological problems posed by the disparity between the given historiography, which accepts the inevitability of the nation-state as the end goal of historical development, and these alluded to developments in Western and Central

Europe, there is the need for alternative thinking and theorizing to guide our future research agendas in political, societal, and economic organization.

In papers presented in Bochum, in 1988, and in Munich, in 1990, I explored some ideas for theorizing beyond the nation-state as it pertained to Ottoman society. Suraiya Faroqhi of Munich University and Fikret Adanir of the Ruhr University in Bochum-Germany are two Ottoman historians who offer fresh thinking on certain aspects of this historiographical phenomenon. They consider particularly the utility of social organization and formation in Ottoman society of the middle centuries (seventeenth and eighteenth) for understanding social and political formations beyond the nation-state; see Suraiya Faroqhi, "Discovering History in the Ottoman Empire," Spring 1990 and F. Adanir, "Christian Churches and the Ottoman Imperial Legitimation in the Balkans (Fifteenth to Nineteenth Centuries)," Spring 1988.

Thinking about Ottoman history beyond the nation-state at the very least, is of use heuristically, since it allows researchers on the middle period, in Ottoman history, to contend with the full complexity of the social and economic experiments of the seventeenth and eighteenth centuries. For example, the phenomenon of corruption in the early modern period is very hard to interpret when viewed through the paradigm of the nation-state. A different attitude toward practices which by the standards of the nation-state would be regarded as corrupt must be attributed in part to the way the Ottoman ruling class viewed public trust. In regarding themselves as entitled to the use of public trust as their personal patrimony, the Ottomans did not act any differently from contemporary European elites.

When describing English bureaucratic practices of the eighteenth and early nineteenth centuries, W. D. Rubinstein ("The End of 'Old Corruption' in Britain," *Past and Present* 101 [1983], 55–86) maintains that practices such as patronage persisted because certain members of the elite had the favor of the crown or belonged to the aristocracy. With regard to some of the differences between premodern and modern concepts, Rubinstein makes the following statement:

> "Many of the patronage offices and places—and, more widely, the system itself—were, I should like to contend, pre-modern and non-rational in

the Weberian sense of failing to obey the rational criteria of all modern bureaucracies which Weber and other sociologists have distinguished as crucial to, and inherent in, the process of modernization. Rewards did not accord with effort or duty; promotion did not occur according to merit or seniority even in a nominal sense; the highest and most lucrative places had the fewest duties and, often, the least raison d'etre. Indeed, the most lucrative and impressive offices frequently had no duties at all, and their holders no objective qualifications for holding them. Succession to responsible office was often determined by hereditary succession to that office or by open sale, criteria which even the Victorian period would find unacceptable. . . . All *modern* bureaucracies and structured organizations, as sociologists have pointed out, obey certain rational criteria of appointment, promotion and hierarchy. Promotion is determined, at least in part, by merit, and offices bear some resemblance to the needs and duties they are supposed to discharge, with the most senior and best rewarded offices in any organization responsible, at least nominally, for taking the most fundamental decisions" (pp. 65–66).

Rubinstein's statements relate to British elite structure. The fact that the practices he describes continued well into the third decade of the nineteenth century indicates that even in the case of England the change over to meritocratic practices was slow, and that the old elites were not destroyed overnight. In other words, the process of transformation to a modern governmental and bureaucratic system was gradual.

14. Mustafa Akdag, *Celali Isyanlari*, Ankara: Ankara Universitesi Basimevi, 1963; idem., *Türkiyenin Iktisadi ve Ictimai Tarihi*, (2 vols. Ankara: Ankara Universitesi Basimevi and Türk Tarih Kurumu, 1959–1971); and William J. Griswold, *Political Unrest and Rebellion in Anatolia 1000–1020/1591–1611*, (Berlin: Klaus Schwarz Verlag, 1983).

15. Halil Inalcik, "Capital Formation in the Ottoman Empire," *Journal of Economic History*, 39.1 (1969), 97–140; Huricihan Islamoglu and Çaglar Keyder, "Agenda for Ottoman History."

Review, 1.1, (1977), 31–56; H. Islamoglu and S . Faroqhi, "Crop Patterns and Agricultural Production Trends in Sixteenth Century Anatolia." *Review*, 2.3, (1979), 401–36. (On these issues, Islamoglu-Inan assured me recently that she has revised her views.)

16. For Egypt, see Kenneth Cuno, "Landholding, Society and Economy in Rural Egypt, 1740–1850." (University of California, Los Angeles, Ph.D. diss., 1985); for south Iraq see Hala Munthir Fattah, "The Development of the Regional Market in Iraq and the Gulf, 1800–1900." (University of California, Los Angeles, Ph.D. dissertation, 1986); and for the same phenomenon in the Mosul region see Dina Rizk Khoury "The Political Economy of the Province of Mosul: 1700–1850," (Georgetown University, Washington, D.C., Ph.D. diss., 1990).

Although lip service is payed to the need for accounting equally for both internal and external factors in the reconstruction of Ottoman history for the period under consideration, hardly anyone has actually demonstrated the fundamental importance of internal dynamics in the understanding of that history. The research efforts by Cuno, Fattah and Khoury suggest ways of thinking about the issues involved, and especially in their focus on the social processes underlying the internal forces for change.

17. Andreas Tietze, (annotated edition and translation of) *Mustafa Ali's Counsel for Sultans 1581* (2 vols. Vienna: Verlag der Österreichischen Akademie der Wissenschaften, 1979–1982), I, 41–65. 'Ali lists the once enforced principles of government; see Appendix A for an outline of his lamentations about the changes he witnessed during his own time.

18. In the words of an order quoted in one of the district court records or *sicilat-i şer'iyye* (in Arabic): "wal-kafalah la tu'khathu min al-yawm fama ba'd, wa-hiya marfu'ah wa-mamnu'ah bimujibi al-hukm al-şarif minal-yawm fama ba'd" (bonding or alibi-taking is not to be taken from this day on, and it [the practice] is lifted and prohibited by the sacred order from this day forward). Also from the same *sicil*: "wa kulu man wajab 'alayh al-jarimah, bi-mujib al-sijil al-shari'i yu'amal biha wa la yu'khathu minhu badal, bal yu'amalu bil-siyasah 'ala mujib al-shar' al-sharif" (On whomever there is settled a crime, in accordance with the sacred *sicil*, he is to be treated [punished]

accordingly, and no commutation or substitution is to be taken, indeed he is to be punished in accordance with the sacred *şar'*). Jerusalem, *sicil*, 16, p. 145, entered in Ramadan 951/December 1544).

19. See the following articles by Rifaat Ali Abou-El-Haj: "The Ottoman Vezir-Pasha Households, 1683–1703: A Preliminary Report," *The Journal of the American Oriental Society*, 94.4 (1972), 438–47; "The Ottoman *Nasihatname* as a discourse over 'Morality'," in *Melanges, Professeur Robert Mantran*, ed. Abdeljelil Temimi (Zaghouan, Tunis: Centre d' Etudes et de Recherches Ottomanes, 1988); "The Nature of the Ottoman State in the Latter Part of the XVIIth Century," in *Ottoman-Habsburg Relations*, ed. Andreas Tietze (Vienna: 1984); in "Power and Social Order: The Uses of the *Kanun*," *Urban Structure and Social Order: The Ottoman City and its Parts*, ed. I. Bierman, Rifaat Ali Abou-El-Haj, and Donald Preziosi (New Rochelle, New York, 1990).

20. Başbakanlik Arşivi, Istanbul, Mühimme defteri 78, p. 491, no. 1252 (1018/1609–1610). I thank Suraiya Faroqhi for this reference.

21. In the first set of sixteenth century *kanunnameler*, for the *liva* of Mosul, the demand for payment in cash of taxes on produce is prohibited. The *kanunname* insists on payment in kind. See "Kanuname-i liva-i Mosul ber mucib-i kanun-i Osmani," Başbakanlik Arşivi, Tapu ve Tahrir Defteri Number 308, p. 5. The 1557 reproduction of the *kanun* for the *liva* reads: "ve galle içun akçe alinmayip, 'ayni ile her cinsden cins-i galle alina" (On the "ghalle" or agricultural produce [the tax] in coin is not to be taken, tax [in kind] is to be taken in the form of the produce on which the tax has been specified). Thus, for instance, there is to be no replacement of a tax on wheat deliveries by deliveries of other crops; nor do peasants need to sell their produce in order to pay their taxes. I presented my general findings on sixteenth century Mosul at Tunis in the spring of 1986. My analysis of the *Mosul liva kanunnameleri* appeared in *La Vie sociale dans les provinces arabes a l'epoque ottomane*, ed. Abdeljelil Temimi (Zaghouan, Tunis: Centre d'Etudes et de Recherches Ottomanes, 1988), pp. 17–39. Compare S. Faroqhi, *Towns and Townsmen of Ottoman Anatolia, Trade, Crafts and Food Production in an Urban Setting* (Cambridge: Cambridge

University Press, 1984), p. 204, for an example of sixteenth and seventeenth century peasants paying half their taxes in cash and the other half in kind.

22. Jerusalem, *sicil*, 16, p. 145, entered in Ramadan, 951/ December, 1544.

23. It is perhaps to the local agents in the provinces acting on behalf of the Istanbul-based high-level officials that we have to look for an explanation of the rise of provincial notables or *ayan*. In most places, the ayan reached their greatest predominance in the eighteenth century. From the ayan were drawn the people who not only regulated and regularized the delivery of revenues. Once established in the provinces, they found it necessary to establish their own police force, intended neither for defense nor for supplementing the centrally located armed forces in Istanbul. The local police force served to guarantee the regular delivery of the revenue which the agents had farmed after successfully bidding for the right of collection at auction. The agents felt entitled not only to the revenue, keeping more and more for themselves, but treated the *miri* land as if it were their private property. Istanbul, in turn, acquiesced. In his study, "Landholding and Society . . . in Egypt," Kenneth Cuno shows the process of conversion of miri land into virtual private property, to exist in eighteenth century Egypt and shows that there were instances that the process was in place earlier.

24. Tietze, *Mustafa Ali's Counsel for Sultans of 1581*, vol. 1, 79–80, 85.

The basic article on the evolution of *timars, ziamets*, and *miri* land into tax-farming or the *malikane* is Mehmet Genç, "Osmanli Maliyesinde Malikane Sistemi," in *Turkiye Iktisat Tarihi Semineri, Metinler-Tartişmalar, 8–10 Haziran 1973*, ed. Osman Okyar and Ünal Nalbantoglu (Ankara: Hacettepe Üniversitesi, 1975), pp. 231–96. For a specific example from the late seventeenth century, see description of the purchase by Rami Mehmed Efendi of a *malikane* and details of the procedures at sale and payments into the treasury, in Rifa'at 'Ali Abou-El-Haj, "The Reisülküttab and Ottoman Diplomacy at Karlowitz" (Princeton University, Ph.D. diss., 1963), pp. 20–59. In support of a similar trend in Algeria for the conversion of *miri* lands into private property see Nasirudin Sa'idouni, in *Dirasat fil-mulkiye al-'Iqariyye fil-'Ahd al-Uthmani*, (Studies in

Land Ownership in the Ottoman Era; Algiers, al-Mu'asasah al-Wataniyah lil-Tiba'a, 1986). The author contends that for Ottoman Algeria, there was a stabilization in landholding and growth in commerce and private property in the period 1600–1800. Sa'idouni shows that by the beginning of the nineteenth century half of all cultivable lands in the North African province had been converted into *vakf* (of all kinds).

While both in their external format and in the structure of their contents the *liva kanunameleri* give the impression of a well-regulated system, the fiscal experiments of the sixteenth and seventeenth centuries reflect an ad hoc and somewhat pragmatic approach to tax extraction, which presages the steady transformation of quite a few Ottoman public lands into private property, a process accelerated in the eighteenth and nineteenth centuries.

After examining eighteen liva kanunnameleri I have come away with the impression that certain offices, at least, were viewed as a source of income rather than as an assortment of specific duties remunerated by a salary. This impression is supported by evidence from the *sicilat-i şer'iye*. For example, for sixteenth century Jerusalem, the *hisba* (market price fixing and supervision of scales and weights) constituted one source of income assigned to the *sancak beyi* of Jerusalem. The sancak beyi sold the right to enforce the hisba to individuals for a limited duration, normally one year. Those who bought the right of hisba regarded the office as a source of income, and not only—or necessarily—a pious act. (Since the quotations are from an Arabic, the transcription follows accordingly.) In the year 1543 (948 A.H.) "istaqart wazifatul hisba bil-Quds al Sharif al-jariyah fi timar . . . Hasan Bey malik-i liwa-i Quds-i Sherif wa madinat al-Khalil . . . 'ala Tajudin b. al-Sukari wa . . . Muhammad b. Zurayq sawiyah 'alayhuma bima laha minal- 'awayid al-qadima . . . fi kuli shahr 75 Qibrisi thahab . . . " (The post of hisba in Jerusalem, with all its lawful incomes and privileges, which is in the timar of Hasan Bey the *mir-i liva* of Jerusalem and the city of Hebron . . . was settled on Tajudin al-Sukari and Muhammad b. Zurayq equally in return for seventy-five gold Qibrisi coins . . .). Jerusalem, sicallat-i şeri-ye, no. 14, p. 185, dated 10. Z. K., 948. Records of similar sales by the *sancak beyis* can be found in ibid., no. 15, p. 389, dated 3. R. I., 950 (for ten months at 5,500 akçe per month); no. 16, p. 9, dated End Jumadi II., 951 (for one year at 40 sultani, gold); no. 18. p. 490, dated 22. Shaval, 953 (for one year at 41 sultani, gold, per month); no. 18, p. 594, dated 27. Z. H., 953 (for one year at 50 qibrisi, gold, per month). Members of the colorful Zurayq family seem to be represented as bidders for the hisba in nearly every one of these transactions. A recent study based on the same Jerusalem court records, is primarily a narrative summery of certain aspects of Jerusalem's economic life in the sixteenth century. Although he refers to the families mentioned above as holders of the "lease" for the hisba, Amnon Cohen, in *Economic Life in Ottoman Jerusalem* (Cambridge: Cambridge University Press, 1989), does not address the issue of the hisba as an office that appeared as a source of income for the governor. Instead, Cohen ennumerates the duties of the *muhtasibs*.

25. I am not unaware of the difference between the de facto and de jure acceptance of private property. The theoretical implications, especially in terms of model building, are quite important. Huri Islamoglu-Inan has commented, in a personal note in 1989, on the changed nature of property holding, but with a focus on the timing of de jure recognition of private property. This focus should not distract from noting the transitional formations reflected in society and state by the de facto transformation of once public lands into private property. Furthermore, the neglect of the process of transformation over time, tends to exaggerate the significance of the formal shift to private property, rendered by the *tapu* land registrations of the middle of the nineteenth century. Some of the transformations are illustrated by 'Ali, *Counsel*; Koçu Bey, *Risale* (Istanbul: Watts Press Edition, 1277/ 1861); Ahmad b. Muhammad b. Omar Khafaji's, *Rihanet al- 'ahiba'* (2 vols.; Cairo, 1967); Naima, *Tarih* (3rd ed.; Istanbul: Amire Press 1281–1281/1864–1866); and Rifa'at 'Ali Abou- El-Haj, *The Rebellion of 1703 and the Structure of Ottoman Politics* (Leiden: Nederlands Historisch Archeologisch Instituut te Istanbul, 1984).

26. Abou-El-Haj, "The Reisülküttab," 47. For rebellions in the Balkans see Bistra Cvetkova, "Problemes du regime ottoman dans les Balkans du seizieme au dix-huitieme siecle," in *Studies in eighteenth century Islamic History*, eds. T. Naff and R. Owen (Carbondale, Illinois: Southern Illinois University Press, 1977); and T. Stoianovich, "The Conquering Balkan Orthodox Merchant," *The Journal of Economic History* 13 (1960), 234–313.

27. 'Ali, *Counsel*, vol. 1, 57, reports the abandonment by the *reaya* of their plots of land and the ensuing loss of the land neglect or çift bozan tax as the reaya settle in the cities as artisans.

28. Koçu Bey, *Risale*, pp. 12–13, comments on the fact that "class" distinctions were beginning to blur, as manifested by the "pretensions" of some *reaya* to belong to other classes. This, Koçu Bey contends, led to *celali* rebellions. See also Andreas Tietze, "Mustafa 'Ali on Luxury and the Status Symbols of Ottoman gentlemen," in *Studia turcologica memoriae Alexi Bombaci dicta*, ed. Aldo Gallotta, Ygo Mazarazzi (Naples, 1982), pp. 577–90.

29. In the course of my research I have come across numerous incidents of social conflict and resistance. Due to the large number of those incidents, only the names of the relevant authors and the titles of their works are cited. L. V. Thomas, *A Study of Naima* (New York, New York University Press, 1972). Mustafa Selaniki, *Tarih*, (Freiburg: Klaus Schwarz Verlag, 1983); Ibrahim Peçevi, *Peçevi tarihi* ed. Fahri Derin and Vahit Çabuk (Istanbul: Enderun Kitabevi, 1980); Katib Çelebi, *Fezleke-i Tarih* (2 vols. Istanbul: Ceride-i Havadis Press, 1286–1287/1869–1871); Mustafa Naima, *Tarih-i Naima* (6 vols. Istanbul: Amire Press, 1281–1283/1864–1866); Silihdar Findiklili Mehmed Aga, *Tarih* (2 vols. Istanbul: Türk Tarih Encümeni Külliyeti, 1928); and Findiklili Mehmed Aga, *Nüsretname* ed. I. Parmaksizoglu (Istanbul: 1962–1969); Mehmed Raşid, *Tarih* (6 vols. Istanbul: 1282/1865); and Defterdar Mehmed, "Zübdet ul-vekayi' " (Istanbul: Süleymaniye kütüphanesi, Esad Efendi 2382).

30. Islamoglu and Keyder, "Agenda for Ottoman History," 31–56.
I first raised the question of social and economic transformations in the seventeenth century in "The Nature of the Ottoman State in the Latter Part of the XVIIth Century." Among others who leave out of consideration the social transformation in Ottoman society commensurate with the transformation in landholding, are Carter Findley, *Bureaucratic Reform in the Ottoman Empire* (Princeton: Princeton University Press, 1980) and most recently Reşat Kasaba, *The Ottoman Empire and the World Economy: The Nineteenth Century* (Albany: State of New York University Press, 1988).

31. Çaglar Keyder, *State and Class in Modern Turkey* (London: New Left Books, 1987).

32. For the early modern period see Brenner, "Agrarian Class Structure and Economic Development in Pre-Industrial Europe." For the later period see especially the discussion of the principal writers in this area by Ralph Miliband, "State Power and Class Interests," *New Left Review* 138 (1983), 57–68. O. Barkan, "The Price Revolution of the sixteenth century: A Turning Point in the Economic History of the Near East." *International Journal of Middle East Studies* 6.1 (1975), 3–28, attributes the crisis in the Ottoman ruling class to a price revolution, generated by European trade and the importation of Spanish silver.

33. Private communication, Andreas Tietze, Vienna, 1985.

34. In a broader investigation of the *nasihatname* literature, I intend to examine the historical specificity of the literary production of each selected example from the sixteenth to the eighteenth centuries and explore the typology of the genre. For a preliminary study, see Rifa'at Abou-El-Haj. "Fitnah, huruc ala al-sultan and nasihat: Political Struggle and Social Conflict in Ottoman Society 1560s–1770s," in *Actes du VIe Symposium du Comite International d'etudes pre-ottomanes et ottomanes*, ed. J.-L. Bacque-Grammont and Emeri van Donzel (Istanbul, 1987).

I explored the emphasis on morality in the genre in "'The Ottoman *Nasihatname* as a Discourse over 'Morality'." There I show that those who lost their monopoly over material resources and those who benefited from the transformation in land holding viewed their conflict in terms of the virtuous *sipahi* against the "other" who in some cases might be a merchant. The discourse between the "virtuous" and the "other" is paralleled by a similar concern in contemporary European political culture, see J. G. A. Pocock, *Virtue, Commerce and History* (Cambridge: Cambridge University Press, 1985), especially pp. 37–71 and 103–23.

35. Twentieth century researchers who have dealt with the *nasihatname* genre as symptoms of decline, either directly or indirectly, can be divided into three generations. Walter Livingston Wright, particularly in his edition of Defterdar Sari Mehmed Paşa, *Ottoman Statecraft, The Book of Counsel for Vezirs and Governors, Nas'ih ül-vüzera ve'l-ümera* (Princeton: Princeton University Press, 1935), and Bernard Lewis, in "Ottoman Ob-

servers of Ottoman Decline," and in *The Emergence of Modern Turkey*, (London, 1976). The second generation is represented by I. Metin Kunt, and to some extent by Madeline C. Zilfi in her most recent work, *Politics of Piety: the Ottoman Ulema in Post-classical Age 1600–1800* (Minneapolis: Bibliotheca Islamica, 1988). I have examined Kunt's work in some detail in "Review Article of *The Sultan's Servants*." The third generation is made up mostly of young scholars just entering the field. They tend to accept the assumptions of the *nasihatname* genre as a given, especially with regard to decline or disruption of norms; they then modify their historical narrative in light of the results of testing the historical accuracy of these assumptions through archival research. For example, Linda Darling, "Ottoman Salary Registers as a Source for Economic and Social History," in *The Turkish Studies Association Bulletin* 14.1 (Spring 1990) 13–34, uncritically uses details from one nasihatname writer's work to define the meaning of archival evidence.

The methodological problem posed by turning to a chronologically late source such as the nasihatname to annotate and define the meaning of an earlier archival one, is obvious. Not only are the sets of sources products of different times but they are usually products of different social contexts. A construct of the conditions that prevailed in the seventeenth century as found in Koçu Bey's *Risale*, cannot define the meaning of the protocols that defined *sipahi* privileges and responsibility that were prevalent in the fifteenth and sixteenth centuries. There is an approach to the use of these two sets of evidence that would obviate their distorted usage. It would require hypothesizing two separate, though immanent processes out of which the archival and nasihatname sources emanate separately.

Darling's "method" is not an innovation: in 1911, the editor of the regulations (*kanunnameler*) issued by Fatih Mehmed in the fifteenth century and Süleyman Kanuni in the sixteenth, turned to a nasihatname of the first half of the seventeenth century for annotation and definition of the concepts and terms found in his publication of the fifteenth and sixteenth century (kanunnameler) regulations. Although writing in the first Ottoman scientific historical journal, the editor of the kanunnameler subordinated his scientific goal in publishing these sources to ideological purposes. That his purpose was the creation of a new Turkish identity, is argued in Abou-El-Haj, "Power and Social Order: The Uses of the *Kanun*."

Many of the recent writers in the field of Ottoman studies manifest a tendency found in the wider field of Middle East studies. They usually convert a contested discourse, for example, political economy or modernization, into a formula. Instead of reconstructing the historical context and therefore the process from which the archival evidence emanates, in order to test the adopted theory, they literally scatter randomly selected evidence onto the theory's structure. The result is an undynamic and unidimensional historical picture based on the evidence that has arbitrarily adhered to the structure. The evidence for the complexity of the social process (of which the archival evidence is an overt product), remains buried in the debris of the archival sources they have ignored.

Cornell Fleischer assigns a place and time for the earliest Ottoman uses of the nasihatname in "From Şehzade Korkud to Mustafa 'Ali: Cultural Origins of the Ottoman Nasihatname," paper presented to the Third International Congress on the Social and Economic History of Turkey, Princeton, New Jersey, August, 1983. I thank him for allowing me to consult his work in manuscript.

36. *Das Asafname des Lutfi Pascha, nach den Handschriften zu Wien, Dresden und Konstantinopel* ed. and trans. Rudolf Tschudi (Berlin: Mayer & Müller, 1910).

37. Here and elsewhere, I review the ways the *nasihatname* genre has been treated in Ottoman studies and suggest how this source can be utilized more fruitfully. My approach is focused on identifying the patterns for which this type of historical material can be used as evidence. For the sixteenth century especially, see the very able work of Cornell H. Fleischer, *Bureaucrat and Intellectual in the Ottoman Empire, The Historian Mustafa 'Ali (1541–1600),* (Princeton, Princeton University Press, 1986), *passim.*

38. In one instance 'Ali says: "wa yakunu lahu 'aynan nazirah . . . (7v)"; (they shall be a seeing eye for him [the ruler]) and "fahaqun 'ala jami' alwara an yamudu als-sultan bilmunasahat . . . (7r)"; (verily it is incumbent upon all to assist the sultan with advice). Translations of the Arabic are mine; the Turkish quotations are from Ali's *Counsel,* ed. Tietze.

39. Compare George Duby, *Les Trois ordres ou l'imaginaire du feodalisme* (Paris, Gallimard, 1978).

40. Abou-El-Haj, *The Rebellion of 1703*, pp. 42, 46–47, 90.

41. The estimate is based on my ongoing study of the *ilmiye* institution ca. 1650–1720. See also the appendix in Abou-El-Haj, "The *Nasihatname* as a Discourse on Morality," pp. 29–30. Zilfi, *Politics of Piety*, pp. 56–60, contends that whereas the trends toward the founding of an ilmiye aristocracy may have started in the seventeenth century, they became institutionalized in the eighteenth. She takes Ahmed III's decree of 1715 as the signal for such an institutionalization. Throughout the work, she takes an institutional approach, leaving the reader at a loss with regard to the process that produced both the phenomena she isolates and the changes that had occurred at particular points in the history of the ilmiye. Thus, for example, there is no convincing explanation for the decree of Ahmed III or its timing in 1715. Did the decree systematize what was already an ongoing process of several decade's duration? Zilfi does not place her analyses within the framework of a sociological theory of bureaucratic growth, nor does she use a comparative approach and draw parallels with a similar institution such as the contemporary Anglican Church in England. Instead she resorts to ad hoc assertions which postulate a static society: "Sometimes the ruthlessness of a Murad IV was a small price to pay for order"; "The coming of the empire had superimposed tenuous lines of authority and patterns of association over the timeless traditional patterns;" "Ottoman society, always traditional, was uncomfortable with the individual." *Politics of Piety*, pp. 92 ff.

42. Halil Inalcik, "Adaletnameler," *Belegeler* II, 3–4 (1965), 49–145.

43. On the regulations proper, see Halil Inalcik, *The Ottoman Empire, The Classical Age 1300–1600* (London: Weidenfeld and Nicolson, 1973), pp. 110–12. On the possible impact of population growth, see Michael Cook, *Population Pressure in Rural Anatolia, 1450–1600* London Oriental Series (London: Oxford University Press, 1972), pp. 1–44.

44. Another contemporary partisan is Defterdar Sari Mehmed Paşa, *Ottoman Statecraft*. Naima, *Tarih*, vol. 1, Preface. For a thorough treatment of this chronicle see Thomas, *A Study of Naima*.

45. See Thomas, *A Study of Naima, passim*.

46. Naima, *Tarih*, vol. 4, 292.

47. For the rebellion of 1703 and an evaluation of the primary sources on it, see Abou-El-Haj, *The Rebellion of 1703*, pp. 3, 33, 36, 43, 89–90.

48. Lutfi Pascha, *Asafname*, pp. 34–35, 43–44.

49. See R. A. Abou-El-Haj, "The Ottoman Vezir and Pasha Households, 1683–1703: A Preliminary Report," *Journal of the American Oriental Society*, 94.4 (1974), 438–47, and idem., *The Rebellion of 1703*, pp. 89–90 and Appendix I, pp. 94–114. What has to be emphasized is the fact that by the end of the seventeenth century changes in the composition of the ruling elite were much more widespread, indicating major trends in sociopolitical and socioeconomic transformation.

50. Elevated to the throne were: Süleyman II: 1099–1102/1687–1691; Ahmed II: 1102–1106/1691–1695; and Ahmed III: 1115–1143/1703–1730. Deposed were: Mehmed IV: 1058–1099/1648–1687; and Mustafa II: 1106–1115/1695–1703.

51. R. A. Abou-El-Haj, "The Nature of the Ottoman State in the Latter Part of the XVIIth Century." For indications of sociopolitical change in the 1580s see Tietze, *Counsel*, vol. 1, 84–85.

52. For references see note 49 above.

53. The sultanic orders for the alienation of public lands were issued by Mustafa II. For a partial text see Abou-El-Haj, *The Rebellion of 1703*, p. 76, n. 285.

54. There are earlier examples of de jure grants of alienation into private property or *temlik*: for an example dated 1049/1639–1640, compare Ömer Lutfi Barkan, "Osmanli Imparatorlugunda bir iskan ve kolonizasyon metodu olarak Vakiflar ve temlikler," *Vakiflar Dergisi*, 2 (1942), 356–57. In this instance, temlik was granted as a first step toward the establishment of a pious foundation. 'Ali and Koçu Bey cite similar cases the late sixteenth and early seventeenth centuries. (Examples cited in Appendixes A and B.)

By the late seventeenth century, one finds numerous examples of the temlik, such as those favoring Feyzullah Efendi and his family, and those favoring Rami Mehmed Efendi. The first example is of a *temlikname* in favor of Feyzullah Efendi, the *şeyhulislam*, and members of his entourage (*Maliye defteri* 9876 for the year 1104/1692–1693, and the other in *Maliye defteri* 9885, pp. 172–73, dated in 1111/1699–1700). The anonymous chronicler reports that for the benefit of Feyzullah, the şeyhülislam, and members of his family, several villages were converted into private property in Anatolia and Syria: "Erzurumda ve Mihalicte me'mur kariyeler hususan kirk elli hasili olan Şamda Balabak muqata'asi ve ziametden tashih olan Mu'athamiyya kariyesei Halep eyaletinde bir kaç pare kariyeler temlik olunmuşidi," Anonymous, "Kitab-i Tevarih-i Sultan Suleyman, Bin doksan dokuz senesinin bin yuz on senesinden söyuler," Ms. Staatsbibliothek, Berlin, Diez A quarto 75, 235b–236a. For Rami Mehmed his awards are cited as: "hisse-i mirileri Hatt-i Humayun Şevketmakrun ile hala Reisulkuttab olan Mehmed Efendi dama mecduhuya temlik olunmagla mülkname-i humayun verilmek içun defter-i mufassaldir . . . " 'Ali Emiri Tasnifi 12.120, in Başbakanlik Arşivi, dated 28 Safer 1112 (August 14, 1700), confirmed in *Maliye defteri* 10148, p. 127, dated Shaban, 1112; the text of a *hüküm* to the *vali*, *molla*, and *muhassil* of Aleppo reiterates the same orders found in the *Maliye* registers, but in a more forceful and telling language asserts the perpetual passage of ownership and total alienation of these public lands to the benefit of the said Rami Mehmed (Efendi) and to his heirs through the generations: " . . . hevas-i humayunuma . . . zikr olunan kura ve mezari' mefruz al-kalem ve maqtu' al-kadem min kul al-vucuh serbest olub; . . . muma ilayh tarafindan zapt olunub naslan ba'da nasl ve far'an ba'da asl anwa'-i vucuh mülkiyyet ile mutasaref olmak üzere mülkname-i humayun 'inayet ve ihsanim olub . . . zikr olunan kura ve mezari'in hudud ve sunurlerine tahdit ve mevcut re'ayasini tahrir içun ferman-i al-işanim sadir olub. . . . " Başbakanlik Arşivi, *Mühimme defteri* III, 531a, dated Mid. Şevval, 1112.

55. A similar case of alienation of public lands, can be cited from late Byzantine history, see Angeliki E. Laiou-Thomadakis, *Peasant Society in the Late Byzantine Empire.* (Princeton: Princeton University Press, 1977). Laiou-Thomadakis treats the last two centuries of the Byzantine Empire but her study is mostly confined to the peasants, villages, and lands of the monasteries of Macedonia; by that time Anatolia had already become Ottoman. Ibid., pp. 3–24.

On the *çiftlik* question compare Bruce McGowan, *Economic Life in Ottoman Europe, Taxation, Trade and the Struggle for*

Land 1600–1800 (Cambridge (UK) and Paris: Cambridge University Press and Maison des Sciences de l'Homme, 1981); Halil Inalcik, "The Emergence of Big Farms, çiftliks: State, Landlords and Tenants," in J.-L. Bacque-Grammont and Paul Dumont eds. *Contributions a l'histoire economique et sociale de l'Empire ottoman,* Collection Turcica III (Louvain: Peeters, 1984); Fikret Adanir, "The Macedonian Question: The Socio-Economic Reality and Problems of Its Historiographic Interpretation," *International Journal of Turkish Studies* 3.1 (Winter 1985–1986), 43–86.

On the transformation of çiftliks in the eighteenth century see the work if Yuzo Nagata, *Some Documents on the Big Farms (Çiftliks) of the Notables in Western Anatolia* (Tokyo: The Institute for the Study of Languages and Cultures of Asia and Africa, 1976) and idem., *Materials on the Bosnian Notables* (Tokyo, 1979). In the last work Nagata suggests that the shifts had already started in the seventeenth century. Khoury, "The Political Economy of the Province of Mosul: 1700–1850" discusses the transfering of villages to the Celili dynasts of Mosul in the eighteenth century.

56. Compare the treatment of "musadere" in *Encyclopedia of Islam*[1] and *Encyclopedia of Islam*[2]; *Islam Ansiklopedisi,* Istanbul, 1940-. Specific historical examples from the seventeenth century are given in Abou-El-Haj's, "Vezir and Pasha Households," pp. 446a–b, n. 36, and *The Rebellion of 1703,* p. 13, n. 35.

57. Yavuz Cezar, *Osmanli Maliyesinde Bunalim ve Digişim Dönemi XVIII yydan Tanzimat'a Mali Tarih* (Istanbul: Alan Yayincilik, 1986), p. 135, refers to the *müsadere* of the later eighteenth century as almost a routine procedure for increasing revenue in times of war.

58. Thus, for example, the wealth of Köprülü Mehmed and that of his first son Fazil Ahmed was passed on to the second son Fazil Mustafa and then to the latter's heirs. The inherited, but intact wealth of this family becomes the target of confiscation when the family was out of political favor. (Silihdar, *Tarih,* II, 567). The Köprülüs, in typical fashion, had tried to provide immunity from confiscation for some of their wealth by translating it into substantial charitable endowments (*evkaf*) (alluded to in *Muhime defteri* 106, 243). The magnitude of these endowments is attested to by the appointment of Şeyhülislam Feyzullah Efendi (d. 1703) as the *nazir,* (guardian-supervisor). Finally,

we have evidence from less well-known vezirial households that the heirs were allowed to continue enjoying the wealth that the head of the family had accumulated. One example is that of Birunsuz Mehmed Bey the son, who was allowed to keep and continue his father's household (*Mühimme defteri* 114, 10b); the same case was also reported in Silihdar (*Nüsretname*, II, 131). By the year 1697–1698, Feyzullah had managed to get himself appointed as guardian-supervisor to more than 100 of the most substantial *vakfs* of the capital (listed in *Maliye defteri* 6006, 8b–9a). This connection gave him not only access to the money accruing from these endowments, but also a hand in their disposition.

As for the confiscations, examples that come to mind from this period are a series of *musadere* decrees which followed the successful overthrow of Mustafa II. Abou-El-Haj, *The Rebellion of 1703*, p. 81, n. 303.

59. Abou-El-Haj, *The Rebellion of 1703*, pp. 28–29, n. 89.

60. Duby, *Trois ordres*, pp. 11ff.

61. The Şeyhulislam was dubbed sahiburreaseteyn, or head, of two branches of government. Abou-El-Haj, *The Rebellion of 1703*, pp. 57–59.

62. One such decree was issued by Dal Taban Mustafa Paşa during his grand vezirate: ibid., 59.

63. Ibid., pp. 82–84.

64. Istanbul; Başbakanlik Arşivi, *Mühimme defteri* 112, dated Şevval and Zulhice, 1113. The decrees were issued to the governors, *kadis* and *müftis* of thirty-five districts, *sancaks*, and *eyalets* of Anatolia and the Balkans. Incidentally, these included every domain that was under the direct "control" of Istanbul. (See Appendix C for the translated text.)

65. See *Mühimme deferi* 111, p. 404, in which the return to certain pagan practices by the Tatars is condemned: "teksim-i emval-i eytamda ve sayir hususlarinda *turah* ta'bir olunur f'il-i kabih terk olunup . . . " (such as the distribution of the property of orphans, and such undesirable acts called "turah", they should be made to abandon . . . ").

The resistance by Ottoman subjects to the territorial compromises, and socioeconomic hardships caused by the demarcations of precise linear borders, Europe's first, agreed to in the treaties of 1699 and 1703, are discussed in R. A. Abou-El-Haj,

"The Formal Closure of the Ottoman Frontier in Europe," *Journal of the American Oriental Society*, vol. 89.3 (1969).

66. Compare Barkan, "Price Revolution," and Halil Inalcik, "Military and Fiscal Transformation in the Ottoman Empire," *Archivum Ottomanicum*, 6, (1980), 283–337; see also Murat Çizakça, "Incorporation of the Middle East into the European World Economy", *Review*, 8.3 (Winter 1985), 353–77.

67. Çizakça, "Incorporation." See also Şevket Pamuk, *100 Soruda Osmanli-Türkiye Iktisadi Tarihi 1500–1914* (Istanbul: Gerçek Yayinevi, 1988) pp. 100–83.

68. Genç, "Malikane," pp. 234–35.

69. When attempting to show that in premodern times, there existed an Ottoman state separate from the ruling class, one may begin with a discussion of the şeri'at. Since the şeri'at was interpreted by the *ulema*, a major theme in Middle Eastern historiography has been the question of political control over the religious and legal specialists in a given Islamic state. Where the Ottomans are concerned, discussion focuses on the degree of autonomy attained by the ulema. Scholars have attempted to determine whether or not the head of the *ilmiye*, the *şeyhülislam*, was free from the sultan's interference, and whether the ruler was more or less free in the formulation of '*örfi* (customary) law. This issue is specious, however, and the assumptions upon which it is based are fallacious, beginning with the assumption that as a class the ulema were separate from the ruling class as a whole. Yet by the second half of the seventeenth century, the most influential elements of the ruling class were to be found within the higher levels of the ilmiye.

Another issue that takes up a great deal of space in twentieth century scholarly literature concerns the supposedly static nature of the canon law (*şeri'at*) and kanun. Here again we can detect the impact (of the principles) of the meritocratic practices of the modern nation-state, and its comparative autonomy from the ruling class. The fascination with the şeri'at's supposed immutability has led too many researchers to devote their time to the study of the various "tricks" devised to make the şeri'at mutable and thereby appropriate for everyday living.

As indicated earlier, the concern of twentieth century scholars with the autonomy of the law is of exceptional interest, since what they are trying to determine is whether or not the institution of ilmiye and its head, the şeyhülislam, were free from outside interference in the formulation of the law. The premise guiding this type of thinking postulates that the şeri'at is an unchanging set of laws. Expressed differently, it would appear that the şeri'at, given its purported origins—God, the Prophet, and the concesus (ijma') of the Muslims—is autonomous. We should not accept the assumptions without prior verification, however. Quite to the contrary; we need to ask why the *mushari'un* or lawmakers insisted on this point. After all, these same lawmakers, or perhaps more accurately "fabricators," defended the immutability of the law in order to ideologically justify the ulema's privileged position in Ottoman society (they were exempt from taxes, exempt from serving in the military and most of the time exempt from confiscations). If we accept without question the premises underlying the Ottoman ulema's position on the issue of immutability of the law, then we acquiesce to the ulema's self-perception, that is we accept the ideology that justifies the privileged place the ulema came to occupy. To avoid this trap I propose that we regard all claims concerning the immutability of the law as a simple cover-up, a device for legitimizing what in fact were ad hoc decisions in the face of real-life, historical situations that required the law as a guide and as a precedent-setting device.

According to the view of many twentieth century specialists, the law serves as a set of rules defining the parameters of change and its delimitations. In place of this view, I propose that we approach the law as a framework to guide practice rather than to limit it. The şeri'at provided precedents where none otherwise would have been, but its principal aim was to meet the demands of the moment, as perceived by those charged with implementing the law. When it came to the actual practice of the şeri'at, its practitioners did change, modify, and legislate as the moment required it, almost invariably in light of the interests of the ruling class, to which the higher echelons of the ulema belonged.

When one examines the manner in which the law was actually applied, it appears that in day-to-day practice, in the sixteenth century as in later periods, innovation was frequent. New solutions were often proposed, something one would not expect to find in a system supposedly unchanging and unchangeable. The observation that the şeri'at was socially dynamic and bound by the moment and circumstance of its utility and application, is as it should be, whether one considers the *sicilat-i şer'iye* (court records) or Ali's recollection of his own experiences of the "violations" of the şeri'at: the way laws are applied in any human society normally indicates how the law fits into the dynamics of the moment of its application. Viewed in this way, and within the context of Ottoman society, the actual formulation, interpretation, and application of the şeri'at were inseparable from the interests of the ruling class.

In two recent studies, I have examined other aspects of the Ottoman kanun. See especially "Power and Social Order: The Social Uses of the Kanun," and "The Ottoman Kanun as an Instrument of Domination," Proceedings of CIEPO, Seventh Symposium, Fall, 1986 Pecs, Hungary.

70. It is important to note that the "feudal" system was not confined to the exploitation of the land but also included other sources of revenue, such as gümrük or excise tax on imports and the hisba dues (payment to market inspector). The diversity of revenue sources explains the success of some members of the ruling class in rapidly accumulating fabulous wealth. Both 'Ali and Koçu Bey note this trend.

71. "Wa laqad khalaqakum atwaran." Nuh, 14, Koran.

72. The conversion of the substantial wealth of the Köprülü family into charitable endowments (evkaf) is indicated in Mühimme defteri 106, p. 243.

73. Istanbul; Başbakanlik Aşivi, Maliye defteri 6006.

74. Consult, for example, Huseyin ibn Ismail Ayvansarayi, Hadikatul- Cevami' (2 vols. Istanbul: Amire Press, 1281/1864–1885).

75. As to further evidence for the fluidity of Ottoman state structure in the late seventeenth century, one might refer to the way charitable endowments were treated when the state treasury was hard pressed for money. Even though vakif incomes were supposedly immune from state intervention, in 1109/1697–1698 contributions were expected from a number of vakif under the supervision of the grand vezir (26 vakifs), şeyhülislam (101 vakifs), der-saadet agasi (77 vakifs), bab-i saadet agasi (34 vakifs), ser hazine-i enderun (4 vakifs), aga-yi saray-i cedid (7 vakifs), and aga-i saray-i 'atik (5 vakifs). Thus, it becomes apparent that charitable foundations were not used solely to provide services according to the will of the founders, but were also made to

serve the "public interest" in a much broader sense. It might even be said that the private interests (whether personal charities or family trusts) of those who set up the endowments were inseparable from the so-called public interest. (See for example *Maliye defteri* 6006 2a–20b, Raşid, *Tarih*, II, 428, and Defterdar Mehmed, "Zubdet . . . ," 345a–b refers to the appropriation of revenue from charitable endowments for public purposes. Abou-El-Haj, *The Rebellion of 1703*, p. 81 points out the way monies were raised for the *cülusiyye* or "coronation gifts" of Ahmed III, including a loan from the orphans' fund, a charitable foundation, located in Istanbul's Bedestan.

76. Perry Anderson, in *Lineages*, resorts to the discussion of the AMP in order to strengthen his assumption, throughout his chapter on the Ottoman realm, that primary factors may account for the differences between the Ottoman/Oriental and the Western European civilizations.

Anderson begins with a promising analysis. As a first step, he discusses the relevance of the AMP concept as applied by Marx and Engels to various historical epochs and areas. He goes on to say that the historical information against which the concept of the AMP was tested has since proven to be defective, or that Marx and Engels misunderstood the evidence. It may be recalled that the AMP is in direct contrast to the mode of production in Europe, which is based on feudalism. The Ottoman/Asiatic mode is characterized by the existence of free peasants (in contrast to European serfs), and by state ownership of land, as well as widespread village autonomy. These factors allow the peasants continued reproduction and permit them to live relatively unmolested by wars and dynastic changes. The AMP is also characterized by one specific administrative problem: because much of the land is infertile, the inhabitants need artificial irrigation, which means that there must be a central authority to adminster the hydraulics. Hence the political dimension is expressed in what has come to be called Oriental Despotism. The AMP thus produces its own peculiar social formation.

Anderson leads us to believe that the concept of the AMP cannot be used as an informing theory to guide our understanding of Ottoman history. Yet he reaches this step in a curious manner, and begs his readers "to bear with him" as he resorts to the use of the term "civilization." (*Lineages*, p. 495.)

It is perhaps not fair to judge Anderson too severely. The secondary sources on which he bases his reconstruction of "Islamic" history are filled with every cliche in the field. Thus, if the portrayal of Ottoman history and society which emerges from Anderson's account is static, it is largely the fault of the secondary literature on which it is based. Anderson, however, must bear his share of the blame, since he does not treat his sources analytically or critically.

No sooner does Anderson abandon the AMP as a framework than he returns to it in the reconstruction of the dynamics for Ottoman history and the social formation which is supposed to be its by-product. It is here that one begins to feel that Anderson is forcing the evidence to fit his structure, thereby making the "history" of the Ottoman Empire conform to the patterns he had discovered for other histories.

As to historical reconstruction in this last section of the book, following the example of his sources, Anderson first launches into a rapid survey of what he calls "Islamic history," beginning with the time of Muhammad the Prophet and selecting typically "Islamic" characteristics which may prove relevant to his discussion of Ottoman history in early modern times. The salient points in this section reiterate every aspect of the AMP which Anderson had outlined previously and deemed irrelevant; namely, that Islamic history is characterized by free peasants; state-owned land; and a civilization which is urban and commercial, and contemptuous of the countryside. Anderson then repeats a series of cliches from the secondary literature, such as: in Islamic civilization, religion is mainly for the benefit of the merchant rather than the peasant or the common man; cities are not autonomous, they lack "coherent internal structure, whether administrative or architectonic" (*Lineages*, p. 504). He continues: "Grown in disorder, lacking plan or charter, the fate of the Islamic cities was normally determined by that of the State whose fortune had conferred their prosperity on them" (p. 595).

In following Anderson's account of the "Islamic" precedents upon which Ottoman society and history were presumably based, the reader is left with shopworn wisdoms current among Middle Eastern specialists, this time concerning the law of private property. Here Anderson is basing himself mainly on the works of F. Lockkegaard (*Islamic Taxation in the Classical Pe-*

riod, Copenhagen, 1950; and J. Schacht, *An Introduction to Islamic Law*, Oxford, 1964):

"The corollary of the legal absence of stable private property in land was the economic spoliation of agriculture in the great Islamic Empires." Initially the land systems of previous "civilizations," were preserved, though without notable additions. But in the long run, a process of beduinization set in. Wide areas of settled peasant cultivation were given up. The "long-run historical curve in this sense was to point steadily downwards" (p. 499).

Then Anderson picks up the Ottoman "attitude" towards labor: "labour was never regarded as so precious by the exploiting class that peasant adscription became a main desideratum. In these conditions, agrarian productivity again and again stagnated or regressed in the Islamic countries, leaving a rural panorama of often 'desolate mediocrity' " (501).

After a discussion of Chinese history, Anderson states: "These elementary contrasts, of course, in no way constitute even the beginnings of a comparison of the real *modes of production* whose complex combination and succession defined the actual social formations of these huge regions outside Europe." Given the differences between the Ottoman Middle East and China, Anderson concludes that one cannot lump these histories and their civilizations together as examples of the same 'Asiatic Mode of Production' " (pp. 548–49).

In his attempt at understanding Ottoman history and society, he had turned to "Islamic" precedents. The unwary reader is left with the understanding that the explication of these precedents is ipso facto sufficient for understanding the specificity of Ottoman history in early modern times. What is missing in Anderson's discussion of the "precedented" institutions, practices, and even culture, are the specifically Ottoman conditions which determined both the reproduction of earlier (Islamic) usages, and the subsequent adaptations and modifications they underwent. Thus the specific dynamics of Ottoman history are totally absent from his approach.

Anderson is not the only analyst who finds it difficult to abandon the idea that the understanding of Ottoman history can be carried out through the analysis of the AMP. Islamoglu and Keyder, in "Agenda for Ottoman History," quite openly attempt the application of the AMP to Ottoman society, basing their argument on the premise that unlike the serfs in Europe, peasants in the Ottoman Empire were "free." But what does it mean for the Near Eastern peasant to be "free" in the circumstances we are discussing? In societies where the AMP held sway, the land was owned publicly, that is, it was not privately held.

Even if the AMP could be applied to the Ottoman Empire and the resultant socioeconomic and sociopolitical formations were commensurate with it, the case could be made for only a short period in Ottoman history, perhaps up to about the second half of the sixteenth century. Sometime in the seventeenth century, however, with the rise of *çiftliks*, *malikane*, and *temlik* practices, with the conversion of many publicly owned lands into private property, and the incipient commercialization of agriculture, the sociopolitical formation experienced major transformations. Economic changes affected surplus extraction and a different social formation was produced. The political struggles and the social unrest of the seventeenth century, reflect, at least in part, an effort by the new social group to fortify its position and thus guarantee its own social reproduction. As an example one might mention the grandees who tried to keep most of the highest positions of government within their families and households. On the other hand, economic changes may have precipitated social dislocation; certain authors, such as Akdag, count the Celali uprisings among the symptoms of these changes.

At the very least we can say that the theory built by Islamoglu and Keyder leads to an oversimplification, which in turn yields a static picture. The treatment of the internal history of Ottoman society over an extended period of time should analyze change caused by complex processes and combine both indigenous factors and external stimulation. One contribution in that direction is Halil Inalcik's recent article, "Rice Cultivation and the *çeltukçi-reaya* System in the Ottoman Empire," *Turcica, Revue d'etudes turques*, 14 (1982), 69–141, where the author finds forced labor in rice cultivation performed by workers who at one point in their history may have been serfs.

77. The approach which assumes that Third World Societies are static still represents a major epistemological problem. The source for this approach is wishful thinking on the part of many Eurocentric researchers. The dilemma in Ottoman historiography is paralleled by writers on the history of early modern South Asia. Frank Perlin outlines the historical issues in "Proto-

industrialization and Pre-colonial South Asia," *Past and Present* no. 98 (February, 1983), 30–95. In "Space and Order Looked at Critically, Non-comparability and Procedural Substantivism in History and the Social Sciences," in *Bifurcation Analysis: Principles, Applications and Synthesis*, ed. M. Hazewinkel et al. (Dordrecht: D. Reidel Publishing Co., 1985), pp. 149–97, Perlin takes up in detail the epistemological problems raised by the Eurocentric researcher's approach.

See note 78 below for examples of Ottoman scholarship that reflect an ahistorical approach to late Ottoman history. One recent paper defending the salutary effect of the *tanzimat* as modernization has been published by Osman Okyar, "A New Look at the Recent Political, Social and Economic Historiography of the Tanzimat," in *Economie et Societes dans l'Empire Ottoman Fin du XVIIIe-Debut du XXe siecle*, ed. Jean Louis Bacque-Grammont and Paul Dumont (Paris: Editions du CNRS, 1983), pp. 33–46. Totally ignoring the historical context for the introduction of the tanzimat, Okyar first criticizes recent modern Turkish scholarly and semipopular analyses of modernization. He condemns writers from the left and from the right, but provides no alternative interpretation except to say that we should accept the introduction of the tanzimat as modernization because that was the only way the Ottoman state could have preserved itself. Behind this view of Ottoman history lies Okyar's perception of the significance of the tanzimat for the development of modernism in republican Turkey. His argument rests on the assumption that the tanzimat was on the one hand a set of ideas and on the other a receptivity to them. Thus, he perceives change as having taken place by exposure to this set of ideas. What is lacking is the reconstruction of the socioeconomic conditions which allowed or disallowed receiving of such ideas. Taken to its logical conclusion, Okyar's argument would lead to the formulation that the tanzimat equals modernization, which in turn means political salvation for the Ottoman successor state. Obviously, Okyar starts with the premise that salvation from the ills of modern Turkey rests with capitalism.

78. As representative examples of the scholarship referred to here I might mention several articles in T. Naff and R. Owen eds., *Studies in Eighteenth Century Islamic History* (Carbondale: Il: Southern Illinois University Press, 1977), and Carter Findley's *Bureaucratic Reform in the Ottoman Empire* (Princeton: Princeton University Press, 1980).

79. The resistance does not necessarily imply rebellion. Since land was still relatively abundant, the peasants' most frequent reaction was to abandon the land and settle in the cities, or else enter into service as mercenaries. Compare Inalcik, "Military and Fiscal Transformation," p. 194ff.

80. A good analysis of the conversion of public land into private property can be found in Ömer Lutfi Barkan, "Türk Toprak Hukuku Tarihinde Tanzimat ve 1277 (1858) Tarihli Arazi Kanunnamesi," in *Türkiye'de Topraka Meselesi, Toplu Eserler*[1] ed. Abidin Nesimi,[1] Mustafa Şahin, Abdullah Özkan (Istanbul: Gozlem Yayinlari, 1980), pp. 291–375.

81. That the peasants continued to be less than sanguine about this change in their status is evidenced by the social unrest in the late nineteenth and early twentieth century, especially in the countryside. Donald Quataert has explored several dimensions of these developments. His most recent study is an article "Machine Breaking and the Changing Carpet Industry of Western Anatolia, 1860–1908." *Journal of Social History*, 19.3, (1986), 473–89.

Gilles Veinstein contends that the *çiftlik* was not nearly as widespread as is sometimes assumed. See his " 'Ayan' de la region d'Izmir et commerce du Levant (Deuxieme moitie du XVIII^c siecle)," *Etudes balkanique*, 12.3 (1976), 71–83.

82. Compare Cemal Kafadar, "A Death in Venice (1575): Anatolian Muslim Merchants Trading in the Serinissima," *Raiyyet Rüsumü, Essays Presented to Halil Inalcik, Journal of Turkish Studies* 10 (1986), 191–218.

83. See especially Hala Fattah, "The Regional Market in Iraq," on the nineteenth century trade between Basra, Najd, and Western Iran on the one hand, and India on the other. Smuggling was rampant then, and aimed at avoiding in particular the duty known as *gümrük*.

84. Compare Fleischer, *Bureaucrat and Intellectual, passim*, and esp. pp. 311–14.

85. Abou-El-Haj, "The Reisülküttab and Ottoman Diplomacy at Karlowitz."

86. For a study of the office of *reisülküttap* in the seventeenth century, see ibid., 20–59. For eighteenth century changes

in this office and the whole problem of cultural exchange, see Ilber Ortayli, "Reforms of Petrine Russia and the Ottoman Mind," *Raiyyet Rüsumü, Essays Presented to Halil Inalcik, Journal of Turkish Studies* 11 (1986), 45–49 and idem., "Ottoman-Habsburg Relations, 1740–1770 and Structural Changes in the International Affairs of the Ottoman State," in *Robert Anhegger Festschrift*, ed. J.-L. Bacque-Grammont et al., (Istanbul: Divit Press, 1988), pp. 287–98.

87. Ayda Arel, *Onsekizinci Yüzyil Istanbul Mimarisinde Batilaşma Süreci* (Istanbul: Istanbul Mimarlik Fakultesi, 1975).

88. Daniel Panzac, *La Peste dans l'Empire Ottoman 1700–1850* (Louvain: Editions Peeters, 1985), pp. 333–38.

89. R. A. Abou-El-Haj, "Physicians and Surgeons of the Eighteenth Century: a contribution to the social history of medicine and modern state formation in the Ottoman Empire," *Festschrift in Honour of Ramkrishna Mukherjee*. Forthcoming.

90. See Engin Akarli, "Provincial Power Magnates in Ottoman Bilad al-Sham and Egypt, 1740–1840," *The Second International Symposium of CERPAO-ACOS, The Social Life of the Arab Provinces and Their Documentary Sources for the Ottoman Period*. (Zaghouan, Tunis, 1988).

91. On the intellectual background of nineteenth century Ottoman-Turkish nationalism, compare Şerif Mardin, *The Genesis of Young Ottoman Thought, A Study in the Modernization of Turkish Political Ideas* (Princeton: Princeton University Press, 1962).

92. Fattah, "The Regional Market in Iraq."

93. On the situation in Spain compare Henry Kamen, *Spain in the Later Seventeenth Century 1665–1700* (London, New York, Longman, 1980) p. 67ff.

94. Although the outline of the argument here may appear overly simple, it nevertheless reflects quite accurately the way change is viewed by social scientists who study the Ottoman nineteenth century. On three occasions, citations are in footnotes 1 and 13 above, I have tried to address the question of Ottoman constitution-making in the second half of the nineteenth century. None of the works consulted seriously postulates that the final decision to adopt a European model for the

first Ottoman constitution was but one among several choices. By not assuming that there were choices, the authors quite literally blot out the intra-elite contest that occasioned the final selection of a European model. That there was a contest is suggested by the (re-)publication in 1860s of several Ottoman works of political culture that were entered into the ensuing discourse over constitution-making. Koçu Bey's *Risale* was one of several such texts.

95. Jack A. Goldstone, "East and West in the Seventeenth Century: Political Crises in Stuart England, Ottoman Turkey, and Ming China," *Comparative Studies in Society and History* 30.1, 1988, 103–42 and Karen Barkey *The State and Peasant Unrest in the Early Seventeenth Century: The Ottoman Empire in Comparative Perspective* (University of Chicago Ph.D. dissertation, 1988) are studies by two sociologists who tackle the issues of comparative history, the crises of the seventeenth century, and state formation in the Ottoman empire. These studies have come too late to my attention for me to seriously discuss them in this study. For sources both authors depend exclusively and uncritically on available secondary and tertiary (textbook) literature in Ottoman studies. Goldstone's work is totally devoid of any references to Ottoman Turkish primary sources and only cites works in English, Barkey's rests on only seven footnote references, in one rapid sequence, to archival sources that she researched. Since neither Goldstone nor Barkey establishes an independent basis for the critical evaluation of the secondary sources on which they base their studies, their outlook on Ottoman state and society repeats the limitations of their highly problematic sources. The epistemological and methodological problems I found in Perry Anderson's *Lineages of the Absolutist State* and Metin Kunt's *The Sultan's Servants*: The Transformation of Ottoman Provincial Government 1550–1650," are repeated here. I will evaluate in detail the studies by Goldstone and Barkey in a forthcoming analysis of Ottoman society in the seventeenth century.

96. Peter Gran, "Studies of Anglo-American Political Economy: Democracy, Orientalism and the Left," in *Theory, Politics and the Arab World*, ed. Hisham Sharabi (New York: Routledge, 1991).

97. Some of the major methodological issues raised here are tackled in Ramkrishna Mukherjee, *Society, Culture, and Development* (New Delhi: Sage Publications India Pvt., 1991).

98. For a discussion of the issue, see Talal Asad, "Multiculturalism and British Identity in the Wake of the Rushdie Affair," *Politics and Society* 18.4 (1990), 455–80; Etienne Balibar and Immanuel Wallerstein, *Race, Nation, Class: Ambiguous Identities* (London: Verso, 1991); Eric Hobsbawn, "Grand Illusions: Perils of the New Nationalism," *Nation* 253.15 (1991), 537, 555–56; and David Held, "Farewell Nation-state," *Marxism Today* 32 (December 1988), 12–17. The most recent treatments of the creation of the nation-state and its place in history include Benedict Anderson's *Imagined Communities: Reflections on the Origin and Spread of Nationalism* (London: Verso, 1983), Eric Hobsbawm's *Nations and Nationalism* (Cambridge: Cambridge University Press, 1980), and Partha Chatterjee's *Nationalist Thought and the Colonial World* (London: Zed Books, 1986).

99. See especially the discussions in Balibar and Wallerstein, *Race, Nation, Class,* and in Asad, "Multiculturalism and British Identity," 455–80.

100. See, for example, *The New Hungarian Quarterly*, 1989–90.

101. See Held, "Farewell Nation-state," in which the author raises the issue of curtailment of sovereignty for the nation-states when capitalist corporations make the globe their market.

102. The issues of Eastern Europe and Russia were discussed by Francis X. Clines, reporting from Yerevan, Armenia (then in the Soviet Union), *The New York Times,* April 15, 1991, and at a symposium held in spring 1990 by the Center for Theory and Comparative History, University of California, Los Angeles.

103. Some of these issues were discussed by Speros Vryonis, Jr., in his *The Decline of Medieval Hellenism in Asia Minor and the Process of Islamization from the Eleventh through the Fifteenth Centuries* (Berkeley: University of California Press, 1971), and by Claude Cahen in his *Pre-Ottoman Turkey: A General Survey of the Material and Spiritual Culture and History, c. 1071–1330* (London: Sidgwick and Jackson, 1968).

104. Halil Berktay, "The Search for the Peasant in Western and Turkish History," *Journal of Peasant Studies* 18.3–4 (1992), 109–84.

105. Eric Hobsbawm, "The Social Function of the Past: Some Questions," *Past and Present* 55 (1972), 2–17.

106. Even recent European historiography is not immune from such distortions. This can be illustrated by the cultivation of amnesia, of which the "Historikertreit" controversy in the German scholarly community is a symptom. This issue has been addressed by Geoff Eley in his article "Nazism, Politics, and Public Memory: Thoughts on the West German Historikerstreit 1986–1987," *Past and Present* 121 (1988), 171–208. The dispute centers on the attempt by certain historians to gloss over the National Socialist period in modern German history as representing an untypical or exceptional phase, without significant links to the total history of Germany.

107. R. A. Abou-El-Haj, "The Social Uses for the Past: Recent Arab Historiography of Ottoman Rule," *International Journal of Middle Eastern Studies* 14.2 (1982), 185–201.

108. How a scholar finds evidence consonant with his or her projection of political or cultural agendas is perhaps best illustrated in Colin Heywood's intellectual biography of the noted European Ottomanist Paul Wittek, "Wittek and the Austrian Tradition," *Journal of the Royal Asiatic Society* 30.1 (1988), 7–25, and in his "Boundless Dreams of the Levant: George-Kreis and the Writing of Ottoman History," *Journal of the Royal Asiatic Society* 31.1 (1989), 32–50.

109. Several studies on the provincial notables are in the work edited by T. Naff and R. Owen, *The Islamic World in the Eighteenth Century* (Carbondale: Southern Illinois University Press, 1977).

110. Ali Ahmida, "For God, Homeland, and Clan: Regional and Social Origins of Collaboration and Anti-Colonial Resistance, Libya 1830–1932" (Ph.D. dissertation, Department of Political Science, University of Washington, 1990).

111. The published tracts are Koçu Bey, *Risale-i Koçu Bey* (Istanbul: N.p., 1861), and Katib Çelebi, *Dusturu 'l-'amel li-islah al-halel* (Istanbul: N.p., 1863). I am in the early stages of my study of Ottoman political culture, especially as it is represented in the

nasihatnamel. In articles and public forums I have examined the various uses and contexts for the production and reproduction of the genre. See especially *"Fitnah, huruc ala al-sultan and nasihat: Political Struggle and Social Conflict in Ottoman Society, 1560s–1770s,"* in *Actes du VIe Symposium du Comité International d'Etudes pré-ottomanes et ottomanes,* ed. Jean-Louis Bacqué-Grammont and Emeri van Donzel (Istanbul: N.p., 1987); "The Social Uses of Culture: The Şeyhulislam versus the 'Historians,' The Genre of Mirror to Princes as a Struggle over Legitimation" (paper presented at the symposium "Legalism and Political Legitimation in the Ottoman Empire," at Rühr University, Bochum, December 1988); "The Ottoman *Nasihatname* as a Discourse over 'Morality,' " in *Mélanges, Professeur Robert Mantran,* ed. Abdeljelil Temimi (Zaghouan, Tunis: Centre d'Etudes et de Recherches Ottomanes, 1988); "The Late Ottoman State and the Discourse over Citizens' Rights and (Ottoman) Turkish National Identity During the Two Constitutional Periods" (paper presented at Middle East Studies Association of America Conference, Toronto, Canada, 1989); "Power and Social Order: The Uses of the *Kanun,"* in *Urban Structure and Social Order: The Ottoman City and Its Parts,* ed. Irene A. Bierman, Rifa'at 'Ali Abou-El-Haj, and Donald Preziosi (New Rochelle, N.Y.: A. D. Caratzas, 1991); and "Ottoman Political Culture of the Seventeenth and Eighteenth Centuries" (paper presented at the Sixth International Conference of Economic and Social History of the Ottoman Empire, Aix-en-Provence, France, 1992).

112. Koçu Bey, *Risale,* 1.

113. Şerif Mardin, *The Genesis of Young Ottoman Thought: A Study in the Modernization of Turkish Political Ideas* (Princeton, N.J.: Princeton University Press, 1962).

114. Robert Devereux, *The First Ottoman Constitutional Period: A Study of the Midhat Constitution and Parliament* (Baltimore: Johns Hopkins Press, 1963); and Roderic H. Davison, *Reform in the Ottoman Empire, 1856–1876* (Princeton, N.J.: Princeton University Press, 1963).

115. See Devereux, *The First Ottoman Constitutional Period,* and Davison, *Reform in the Ottoman Empire.*

116. Bernard Lewis, *The Emergence of Modem Turkey* (London: Oxford University Press, 1961).

117. Hala Munthir Fattah, "The Development of the Regional

Market in Iraq and the Gulf, 1800–1900" (Ph.D. dissertation, University of California, 1986).

118. Dina Rizk Khoury, "The Political Economy of the Province of Mosul: 1700–1850" (Ph.D. dissertation, Georgetown University, 1987).

119. André Raymond, *Grandes villes arabes à l'époque ottomane* (Paris: Sindbad, 1985).

120. Lecture by Raymond on the Ottoman Arab cities in Los Angeles, California, in spring 1990.

121. Tülay Artan, "Architecture as a Theatre of Life: Profile of the Eighteenth Century Bosphorus" (Ph.D. dissertation, Massachusetts Institute of Technology, 1989).

122. For India, see Ramkrishan Mukherjee, *The Rise and Fall of the East India Company* (New York: Monthly Review Press, 1974), 140–212; and Frank Perlin, "Proto-industrialization and Pre-colonial South Asia," *Past and Present* 98 (1983), 30–95. For China, see Paul A. Cohen, *Discovering History in China: American Historical Writing on the Recent Chinese Past* (New York: Columbia University Press, 1984). For an African view, see A. Adu Boahen, *African Perspectives on Colonialism* (Baltimore: Johns Hopkins University Press, 1987). For the late Habsburg Empire, see Margaret Olin, "Alois Riegl: The Late Roman Empire in the Late Habsburg Empire" (paper presented at the symposium "The Hapsburg Legacy: National Identity in Historical Perpsective," held at the Institute of Germanic Studies, London, September 1992; I thank the author for allowing me to read this paper).

123. "Dönme," in *Islam Ansiklopedisi*, 1941–; Gershom Scholem, *Sabbatai Sevi: The Mystical Messiah, 1626–1676* (Princeton, N.J.: Princeton University Press, 1973); and Traian Stoianovitch, "The Conquering Balkan Orthodox Merchant," *The Journal of Economic History* 20 (1960), 234–313.

124. Stoianovitch, "The Conquering Balkan Orthodox Merchant."

125. Rifa'at 'Ali Abou-El-Haj, *Formation of the Modern State: The Ottoman Empire Sixteenth to Eighteenth Centuries* (Albany: State University of New York Press, 1991).

126. Abou-El-Haj, *Formation of the Modern State.*

127. Metin I. Kunt, "Ottoman Names and Ottoman Ages," *Journal of Turkish Studies* 10 (1986), 227–34.

128. Social and intellectual transformations to parallel those noted here are also recorded by Ekmelüddin Ihsanoğlu, "Some Critical Notes on the Introduction of Modem Sciences to the Ottoman State and the Relation Between Science and Religion up to the End of the Nineteenth Century," *Proceedings of CIEPO, Fourth Symposium*, ed. Jean-Louis Bacqué-Grammont and Emeri van Donzel (Istanbul: N.p., 1987). The fluidity of social processes in Egyptian society of the eighteenth and early nineteenth centuries is noted in Peter Gran, *Islamic Roots of Capitalism: Egypt, 1760–1840* (Austin: University of Texas Press, 1979). That the shift in the economy had commensurate administrative and social implications is manifest in the fluidity which characterized the application of the social and economic regulations or *kanun* as noted by Abou-El-Haj, "The Ottoman Kanun as an Instrument of Domination," *Proceedings of CIEPO, Seventh Symposium*, fall 1986, Pecs, Hungary. The transformation in the use of the *kanun* in Ottoman political culture during the last century of Ottoman rule is discussed by Abou-El-Haj in "Power and Social Order: The Uses of the *Kanun.*" The political culture of Western Europe during the same era equally reflects the shift to private property and liquidity (in the form of money). In the Ottoman case this parallel shift resonates culturally in a discourse over morality and virtue, as discussed by Abou-El-Haj, in "The Ottoman *Nasihatname* as a Discourse over 'Morality.' "

129. A. K. Sanjian and Andreas Tietze, *Eremya Chelebi Komurian's Armeno-Turkish Poem "The Jewish Bride"* (Wiesbaden: Akadémiai Kiadó, 1981); and Andreas Tietze's rendition in Latin letters of Vartan Pasha's *Akabi Hikayesi*(Istanbul: Eren Yayinevi, 1991), an 1851 novel published in Armenian script, but in the Ottoman Turkish language: *Vartan Paşa, Akabi Hikâyesi: ilk Trke Roman (1851)*, ed. Andreas Tietze (Istanbul: Eren Yayinevi, 1991).

130. It is therefore unlike the approach adopted by Elie Kedourie in *Nationalism in Asia and Africa* (London: Weidenfeld and Nicolson, 1970). Kedourie is guided by the proposition that former Ottoman subjects were incapable of undergoing the liberal experiment and therefore were the least likely to benefit from the formation of a nation-state. In a discussion of this phenomenon, Parthee Chatterjee points out that Kedourie believes in "the essential fairness and nobility of the true principles of empire" *(Nationalist Thought and the Colonial World, 7)*. Chatterjee adopts a different angle from which to handle this issue.

Bibliography

Unpublished Sources (archival)

Istanbul: Başbakanlik Arşivi (State Central Archives): 'Ali Emiri tasnifi 12120; Maliye defterleri: 6006, 9876, 9885, 10148; Mühimme defterleri: 78, 106, 111, 114; Tapu ve Tahrir defteri, 308.

Jerusalem, sicilat-i şeri'ye, (kadi court records) nos. 14, 16, 18 (all from the sixteenth century). (Permission for the use of these archives was granted by the Chief Justice of Jordan, kadi al-kudat, in 1964–1965.)

Unpublished Sources (libraries)

Anonymous, Kitab-i Tevarih-i Sultan Suleyman, bin doksan dokuz senesinin bin yuz on senesinden soyuler." MS. Staatbibliothek (Berlin), Diez A Quarto 75.

Defterdar Sari Mehmed Paşa, "Zubdetul-vekayi'," (Istanbul, Suleymaniye kutuphanesi, Esad Efendi 2382).

Silihdar Mehmed, "Nüsretname," MS. Istanbul, Beyazit Umumi Kutuphanesi, 2369.

Şeyhi, "Vakayiul-fuzela," (unpublished manuscript, Vienna, Nationalbiliothek, H.O., 126) 2 vols.

Printed Sources

Abou-El-Haj, Rifa'at 'Ali. "Trade, Commerce and Society in the Arab Provinces of the Ottoman Empire, based on XVIth century liva kanunnameler." In manuscript.

—————."Efficient Consideration For Theorizing Beyond the Nation-State: The Case of Early Modern and Modern Ottoman Society." Unpublished paper presented at a conference on "The State, Decentralization and Tax Farming (1500–1850), The Ottoman Empire, India and Iran." Munich, Germany, Spring, 1990.

—————."The Late Ottoman State and the Discourse over Citizens' Rights and (Ottoman) Turkish National Identity During the Two Constitutional Periods." Unpublished paper, presented at Middle East Studies Association of America Conference, Toronto, Canada, 1989.

—————."The Social Uses of Culture: The Şeyhulislam Versus the 'Historians.' The Genre of Mirror to Princes as a struggle over legitimation: (With a contribution to historiography and methodology in Ottoman history." Unpublished paper given at symposium, Legalism and Political Legitimation in the Ottoman Empire, Bochum, Rühr University, December, 1988.

—————."Methods, Methodology, and Historiography in Ottoman and Middle East Studies since *Orientalism*." In manuscript.

—————."Physicians and Surgeons of the Eighteenth Century: A Contribution to the Social History of Medicine and Modern State Formation in the Ottoman Empire." In manuscript.

Abul-Hajj, Rif'at 'Ali. " 'Ara' 'Arabiyyah 'an al-Inhitat al-'Uthamni," (Arab views of Ottoman decline). *Proceedings of the International Conference on Arab Thought in the Ottoman Period.* In press.

Abou-El-Haj, Rifa'at Ali. "Power and Social Order: The Uses of the *Kanun*," *Urban Structure and Social Order: The Ottoman City and Its Parts*, ed. I. Bierman, R. A. Abou-El-Haj, and D. Preziosi. In press.

————."The Ottoman Kanun as an Instrument of Domination." *Proceedings of CIEPO, Seventh Symposium, Fall, 1986 Pecs, Hungary*. In press.

————."The Ottoman *Nasihatname* as a Discourse over 'Morality'," in *Melanges, Professeur Robert Mantran*, ed. Abdeljelil Temimi (Zaghouan, Tunis: Centre d' Etudes et de Recherches Ottomanes, 1988).

————."Review of V. Volkan and Norman Itzkowitz, *Atatürk*," *International Journal of Turkish Studies* 4.1 (1987), 149–51;

————."Review Article: I. Metin Kunt, *The Sultan's Servants*: The Transformation of Ottoman Provincial Government 1550–1650." *Osmanli Ariştirmalari* (The Journal of Ottoman Studies) 6 1986 pp. 221–46.

————."Fitnah, huruc ala al-sultan and nasihat: Political Struggle and Social Conflict in Ottoman Society 1560s–1770s." *Actes du VIe Symposium du Comite International d'etudes pre-ottomanes et ottomanes*, ed. J.-L. Bacque-Grammont and Emeri van Donzel, Istanbul, 1987.

————."The Nature of the Ottoman State in the Latter Part of the XVIIth Century," in *Ottoman-Habsburg Relations*. ed. A. Tietze. Vienna, 1984.

————."Taxation, Trade, Production and Society in 16th Century Mosul." in *La vie sociale dans les provinces arabes a l'epoque ottomane*. Vol 3. ed. Abdeljelil Temimi. Zaghouan, Tunis, 1988, pp. 17–39.

————.*The Rebellion of 1703 and the Structure of Ottoman Politics*. Leiden: Nederlands Historisch Archeologisch Institut te Istanbul, 1984.

————."The Social Uses for the Past: Recent Arab Historiography of Ottoman Rule." *International Journal of Middle East Studies* 14.2 (1982), 185–201 (a French translation appeared simultaneously in, *Maghreb Machrek* 97. 1982).

————."An Agenda for Research in History: The History of Libya between the Sixteenth and Nineteenth Centuries." *International Journal of Middle East Studies* 15. 1983.

————."Amnon Cohen and Bernard Lewis, *Population and Revenue in the Towns of Palestine in the Sixteenth Century.*" *The Muslim World* 78, (1980), pp. 156–58.

————."Review of Thomas Naff and Roger Owen, eds. *Studies in Eighteenth Century Islamic History.*" *The Historian* XLI.4 (1979), pp. 790–91.

————."Stanford J. Shaw, *The Ottoman Empire*, Vol. I." *American Historical Review* 82.4 (1977), pp. 1029a–b.

————."The Ottoman Vezir and Pasha Households, 1683–1703: A Preliminary Report," *Journal of the American Oriental Society* 94.4, 1972, pp. 438–47.

————."The Formal Closure of the Ottoman Frontier in Europe," *Journal of the American Oriental Society.* Vol 89.3, 1969.

————.*The Reisülküttab and Ottoman Diplomacy at Karlowitz.* Princeton University, Ph.D. diss., 1963.

Adanir, Fikret. "Christian Churches and the Ottoman Imperial Legitimation in the Balkans (Fifteenth to Nineteenth Centuries)," Spring, 1988. I thank the author for allowing me to read this paper in manuscript.

————."The Macedonian Question: The Socio-Economic Reality and Problems of its Historiographic Interpretation." *International Journal of Turkish Studies* 3.1 (Winter 1985–86), 43–86.

Akarli, Engin. "Provincial Power Magnates in Ottoman Bilad al-Sham and Egypt, 1740–1840," in *La vie sociale dans les provinces arabes a l'epoque ottomane.* Vol 3. ed. Abdeljelil Temimi. Zaghouan, Tunis, 1988.

Akdag, Mustafa. *Celali Isyanlari.* Ankara: Ankara Universitesi Basimevi, 1963.

————.*Türkiyenin Iktisadi ve Ictimai Tarihi.* 2 vols. Ankara: Ankara Üniversitesi and Türk Tarih Kurumu, 1959–1971.

Anderson, Perry. *Lineages of the Absolutist State.* London: NLB, 1974.

Ayda Arel. *Onsekizinci Yüzyil Istanbul Mimarisinde Batilaşma Süreci.* Istanbul: Istanbul Mimarlik Fakultesi, 1975.

Artan, Tülay. "Architecture as a Theatre of Life: Profils of the Eighteenth Century Bosphorus." Cambridge: Massachusetts Institute of Technology, Ph.D. diss., 1989.

Aston, T. S. ed. *Crisis in Europe 1560–1660*. London: Routledge and Kegan Paul, 1965.

Aston, T. H. and C. H. E. Philip. *The Brenner Debate, Agrarian Class Structure and Economic Development in Pre-Industrial Europe*. Cambridge: Cambridge University Press, 1985.

Ayvansarayi, Huseyin ibn Ismail. *Hadikatul- Cevami'*. 2 vols. Istanbul: Amire Press, 1281/1864–1885.

Barkan O. "The Price Revolution of the Sixteenth Century: A Turning Point in the Economic History of the Near East." *International Journal of Middle East Studies* 6.1 (1975), pp. 3–28.

———.*Türkiyede Toprak Meselsi*. Istanbul: Gözlem Yayilari, 1980.

———."Osmanli Imparatorlugunda bir iskan ve kolonizasyon metodu olarak Vakiflar ve temlikler." *Vakiflar Dergis*, 2 (1942), pp. 356–57.

———."Türk Toprak Hukuku Tarihinde Tanzimat ve 1277 (1858) Tarihli Arazi Kanunnamesi," in *Türkiye'de Topraka Meselesi, Toplu Eserler*[1], ed. Abidin Nesimi, Mustafa Şahin, and Abdullah Özkan. Istanbul: Gozlem Yayinlari, 1980, pp. 291–375.

Barkey, Karen. "The State and Peasant Unrest in Early Seventeenth Century: The Ottoman Empire in Comparative Perspective." University of Chicago, Ph.D. diss., 1988.

Berktay, Halil. "Centralization and Decentralization in the State-fetishist Perspective of the Twentieth Century Turkish Historiography." Paper given at conference on comparative Ottoman, Safavi, and Mogul civilizations, at Munich, Germany, Spring, 1990.

Brenner, Robert. "Agrarian Class Structure and Economic Development in Pre-industrial Europe," in T. H. Aston and C. H. E. Philpin eds. *The Brenner Debate*. Cambridge: Cambridge University Press, 1985.

————."Reply," in T. H. Aston and C. H. E. Philpin eds., *The Brenner Debate*. Cambridge: Cambridge University Press, 1985.

Carr, E. H. *What is History?* New York: Alfred A. Knopf, 1972.

Katib Çelebi. *Fezleke-i Tarih*. 2 vols. Istanbul: Ceride-i Havadis Press, 1286–1287/1869–1871.

Cezar, Yavuz. *Osmanli Maliyesinde Bunalim ve Degişim Dönemi XVIIIyydan Tanzimat'a Mali Tarih*. Istanbul: Alan Yayincilik, 1986.

Çizakça, Murat. "Incorporation of the Middle East into the World Economy." *Review* 8.3 (Winter, 1985), pp. 353–77.

Cohen, Amnon. *Economic Life in Ottoman Jerusalem*. Cambridge: Cambridge University Press, 1989.

Cook, Michael. *Population Pressure in Rural Anatolia, 1450–1600*. London Oriental Series. Vol. 27. London: Oxford University Press, 1972.

Cuno, Kenneth. "Landholding, Society and Economy in Rural Egypt, 174–1850." University of California, Los Angeles, Ph.D. diss., 1985.

Cvetkova, Bistra "Problemes du regime ottoman dans les Balkans du seizieme au dix-huitieme siecle," in *Studies in Eighteenth Century Islamic History*, ed. T. Naff and R. Owen Carbondale, Illinois: Southern Illinois University Press, 1977, pp. 165–83.

Darling, Linda. "Ottoman Salary Registers as a Source for Economic and Social History." *The Turkish Studies Association Bulletin* 14.1 (Spring, 1990), pp. 13–34.

Davison, Roderic H. *Reform in the Ottoman Empire 1856–1876*. Princeton: Princeton University Press, 1963.

Devereux, Robert. *The First Ottoman Constitutional Period*. Baltimore: Johns Hopkins University Press, 1963.

Duby, George. *Les Trois ordres ou l'imaginaire du feodalisme*. Paris: Gallimard, 1978.

Encyclopedia of Islam[1]. Ed. A. J. Wensinck et al. 4 vols. and Supplement, Leiden, 1913–1938.

Encyclopedia of Islam[2]. New Edition, ed. Bernard Lewis et al., Leiden, 1954–.

Faroqhi, S. "Discovering History in the Ottoman Empire," Spring, 1990. I thank the author for allowing me to read this paper in manuscript.

––––––.*Towns and Townsmen of Ottoman Anatolia, Trade, Crafts and Food Production in an Urban Setting.* Cambridge: Cambridge University Press, 1984.

Fattah, Hala Munthir. "The Development of the Regional Market in Iraq and the Gulf, 1800–1900." University of California, Los Angeles, Ph.D. diss., 1986.

Findley, Carter. *Bureaucratic Reform in the Ottoman Empire.* Princeton: Princeton University Press, 1980.

Fleischer, Cornell H. *Bureaucrat and Intellectual in the Ottoman Empire, The Historian Mustafa 'Ali (1541–1600).* Princeton: Princeton University Press, 1986.

Fleischer, Cornell H. "From Şehzade Korkud to Mustafa 'Ali: Cultural Origins of the Ottoman Nasihatname." Paper presented to the Third International Congress on the Social and Economic History of Turkey, Princeton, New Jersey, August, 1983. I thank the author for allowing me to consult his work in manuscript.

Genç, Mehmet. "Osmanli Maliyesinde Malikane Sistemi," in Osman Okyar and Ünal Nalbantoglu, eds. *Türkiye Iktisat Tarih Semineri, Metinler-Tartişmalar.* 8–10 Haziran 1973. Ankara: Hacetepe Üniversitesi, 1975, pp. 231–96.

Gibb, H. A. R. and Harold Bowen. *Islamic Society and the West.* Vol. I, part 1. London: Oxford University Press, 1950.

Goldstone, Jack A. "East and West in the Seventeenth Century: Political Crises in Stuart England, Ottoman Turkey, and Ming China." *Comparative Studies in Society and History* 30.1, 1988, pp. 103–42.

Griswold, William J. *Political Unrest and Rebellion in Anatolia 1000–1020/1591–1611.* Berlin: Klaus Schwarz Verlag, 1983.

Howard, Douglas A. "Ottoman Political Literature and the Concept of 'Decline' in the Sixteenth and Seventeenth

Centuries." Forthcoming. I thank the author for allowing me to consult his work in manuscript.

———."The Ottoman Timar System and Its Transformation: 1563–1656." Bloomington, Indiana University, Ph.D. diss., 1987. I thank the author for allowing me to consult his work in manuscript.

Inalcik, Halil. "The Emergence of Big Farms, *çiftliks*: State, Landlords and Tenants," in J.-L. Bacque-Grammont and Paul Dumont, eds., *Contributions a l'histoire economique et sociale de l'Empire ottoman*. Collection Turcica III, Louvain: Peeters, (1984), pp. 105–26.

———."Rice Cultivation and the *çeltükci-reaya* System in the Ottoman Empire." *Turcica, Revue d'etudes turques* 14 (1982), 69–141.

———."Military and Fiscal Transformation in the Ottoman Empire." *Archivum Ottomanicum*, 6, (1980), 283–337.

———."Impact of the *Annales* School on Ottoman Studies and New Findings." *Review* (Journal of the Fernand Braudel Center. State University of New York, Binghamton, New York) 1.3 and 4, (1978), 69–96.

———.*The Ottoman Empire, The Classical Age 1300–1600*. London: Wiedenfeld and Nicolson, 1973.

———."Capital Formation in the Ottoman Empire." *Journal of Economic History* 39.1 (1969), 97–140.

———."Adaletnameler." *Belegeler* II, 3–4 (1965), pp. 49–145.

Islam Ansiklopedisi. Istanbul, 1940–.

Islamoglu-Inan, Huri. *The Ottoman Empire and the World-Economy*. Cambridge: University Press, 1987.

Islamoglu, H. and S. Faroqhi. "Crop Patterns and Agricultural Production Trends in Sixteenth Century Anatolia." *Review*, 2.3 (1979), pp. 400–36.

Islamoglu, Huricihan and Çaglar Keyder. "Agenda for Ottoman History." *Review* 1.1, (1977), pp. 31–55.

———."Les Paysans, Le Marche et l'Etat en Anatolie Au XVIe Siecle." *Annales, Economies, Societes, Civilizations*. Septembre-Octobre, 1988, pp. 1025–43.

Itzkowitz, Norman. "Eighteenth Century Ottoman Realities." *Studia Islamica* 16, (1962).

Kafadar, Cemal. "A Death in Venice (1575): Anatolian Muslim Merchants Trading in the Serinissima." *Raiyyet Rüsumü, Essays Presented to Halil Inalcik, Journal of Turkish Studies* 10 (1986), pp. 191–218.

Kamen, Henry. *Spain in the Later seventeenth century 1665–1700.* London: New York, Longman, 1980.

Kasaba, Reşat. *The Ottoman Empire and the World Economy, The Nineteenth Century.* Albany: State University of New York Press, 1988.

Keyder, Çaglar. *State and Class in Modern Turkey.* London: New Left Books, 1987.

Khafaji, Ahmad b. Muhammad b. Omar. *Rihanet al-'ahiba'.* 2 vols. Cairo, 1967.

Khoury, Dina Rizk. "The Political Economy of the Province of Mosul: 1700–1850." Georgetown University, Washington, D.C., Ph.D. diss., 1987.

Klaveren, Jacob van. "Fiscalism, Mercantilism and Corruption," in *Revisions in Mercantalism.* ed. D. C. Coleman. London: Methuen, 1969, pp. 140–62.

Koçu Bey. *Risale-i Koçu Bey.* Istanbul, Watts Press, 1277/1861.

Kunt, I. Metin. *The Sultan's Servants. Transformation of Ottoman Provincial Government 155–1650.* New York: Columbia University Press, 1983.

Ladurie, Emmanuel Le Roy. "Les masses profondes: La paysannerie," in *Histoire economique et sociale de la France.* Vol 2. *Paysannerie et croissance.* eds. E. Le Roy Ladurie and Michel Morineau. Paris: PUF 1977, pp. 483–872.

Lefebvre, Henri. "Marxism Exploded." *Review* IV.1, (1980), pp. 19–32.

Lewis, Bernard. *The Emergence of Modern Turkey.* London: Oxford University Press, 1969.

———."Ottoman Observers of Ottoman Decline." *Islamic Studies* 1 (1962), pp. 72–87.

Lockkegaard, F. *Islamic Taxation in the Classical Period.* Copenhagen, 1950.

Lütfi Pascha. *Das Asafname des Lutfi Pascha, nach den Handschriften zu Wien, Dresden und Konstantinopel.* Ed. and trans. Rudolf Tschudi. Berlin: Mayer & Müller, 1910.

Mardin, Şerif. *The Genesis of Young Ottoman Thought, A Study in the Modernization of Turkish Political Ideas.* Princeton: Princeton University Press, 1962.

McGowan, Bruce. *Economic Life in Ottoman Europe, Taxation, Trade and the Struggle for Land 1600–1800.* Cambridge (UK) and Paris: Cambridge University Press and Maison des Sciences de l'Homme, 1981.

Mehmed Aga, Silihdar Findiklili. *Tarih.* 2 vols. Istanbul: Türk Tarih Encümeni Külliyeti, 1928.

———.*Nüsretname,* Translation into Modern Turkish by Ismet Parmaksizoglu, Istanbul, 1962–1969.

Mehmed Paşa, Defterdar Sari. *Ottoman Statecraft, The Book of Counsel for Vezirs and Governors, Nas'ih ül-vüzera ve'l-ümera.* Ed. and trans. Walter Livingston Wright. Princeton: Princeton University Press, 1935.

Miliband, Ralph. "State Power and Class Interests." *New Left Review* 138 (1983), pp. 57–68.

Mousnier, Roland. *Peasant Uprisings in Seventeenth Century France, Russia and China.* London: George Allen and Unwin Ltd, 1971.

Naff, T. and R. Owen. *Studies in Eighteenth Century Islamic History.* Carbondale: Illinois. Southern Illinois University Press, 1977. (See also my review of this work in *The Historian,* 1979.)

Nagata, Yuzo. *Some Documents on the Big Farms (çiftliks) of the Notables in Western Anatolia (Chiftliks).* Tokyo: Institute for the Study of Languages and Cultures of Asia and Africa, 1976.

———. *Materials on the Bosnian Notables.* Tokyo: Institute for the Study of Languages and Cultures of Asia and Africa, 1979.

Naima, Mustafa. *Tarih*. 6 vols. 3rd ed. Istanbul: Amire Press, 1281–1283/1864–1866.

Okyar, Osman. "A New Look at the Recent Political, Social and Economic Historiography of the Tanzimat," in *Economie et Societes dans l'Empire Ottoman Fin du XVIIIe-Debut du XXe siecle*. Ed. Jean Louis Bacque-Grammont and Paul Dumont. Paris: Editions du CNRS, 1983, pp. 33–46.

Ortayli, Ilber. "Ottoman-Habsburg Relations, 1740–1770 and Structural Changes in the International Affairs of the Ottoman State," in *Robert Anhegger Festschrift*. Ed. J.-L. Bacque-Grammont et al. Istanbul: Divit Press, 1988, pp. 287–98.

————."Reforms of Petrine Russia and the Ottoman Mind." *Raiyyet Rüsumü, Essays Presented to Halil Inalcik, Journal of Turkish Studies* 11 (1986), pp. 45–49.

Owen, Roger. "The Middle East in the Eighteenth Century—On Islamic Decline: A critique of Gibb and Bowen's *Islamic Society and the West*." *Review of Middle East Studies* 1 (1975), 101–12.

Pamuk, Şevket. *100 Soruda Osmanli-Turkiye Iktisdi Tarihi 1500–1914*. Istanbul: Gerçek Yayinevi, 1988.

Panzac, Daniel. *La Peste dans l'Empire Ottoman 1700–1850*. Louvain: Editions Peeters, 1985.

Parker, Geoffrey and Lesley M. Smith, eds. *The General Crisis of the Seventeenth Century*. London: Routledge and Kegan Paul, 1978.

Peçevi, Ibrahim. *Peçevi Tarihi*. Fahri Derin and Vahit Çabuk, ed. Istanbul: Enderun Kitabevi, 1980.

Perlin, Frank. "Proto-industrialization and Pre-colonial South Asia." *Past and Present* no. 98 (February, 1983), pp. 30–95.

————."Space and Order Looked at Critically, Noncomparability and Procedural Substantivism in History and the Social Sciences," in *Bifurcation Analysis: Principles, Applications and Synthesis*. Ed. M. Hazewinkel et al. Dordrecht: D. Reidel Publishing Co., 1985, pp. 149–97.

Pocock, J. G. A. *Virtue, Commerce and History*. Cambridge: Cambridge University Press, 1985.

Porchnev, Boris. *Les Soulevements populaires en France au XVIIe siecle.* Paris: Flammarion, 1972.

Quataert, Donald. "Machine Breaking and the Changing Carpet Industry of Western Anatolia, 1860–1908." *Journal of Social History* 19.3, (1986), pp. 473–89.

Raşid, Mehmed. *Tarih.* 6 vols. Istanbul, 1282/1865.

Rubinstein, W. D. "The End of 'Old Corruption' in Britain." *Past and Present* 101, 1983, 55–86.

Sa'idouni, Nasirudin. *Dirasat fil-mulkiye al-'Iqariyye fil-'Ahd al-Uthmani.* (Studies in Land Ownership in the Ottoman Era) Algiers: al-Mu'asasah al-Wataniyah lil-Tiba'a, 1986.

Schacht, J. *An Introduction to Islamic Law.* Oxford: Oxford University Press, 1964.

Selaniki, Mustafa. *Tarih.* Freiburg: Klaus Schwarz Verlag, 1983.

Stoianovich, T. "Land Tenure and Related Sectors of the Balkan Economy, 1600–1800." *Journal of Economic History* 13, (1953), pp. 398–411.

———."The Conquering Balkan Orthodox Merchant." *Journal of Economic History* 20, (1960), pp. 234–313.

Stone, Lawrence. *The Causes of the English Revolution 1526–1642.* London: Routlege and Kegan Paul, 1972.

Sureya, Mehmed. *Sicil-i Osmani.* 4 vols. Istanbul, 1308.

Tietze, Andreas. "Mustafa 'Ali on Luxury and the Status Symbols of Ottoman gentlemen," in *Studia turcologica memoriae Alexi Bombaci dicta.* Ed. Aldo Gallotta and Ygo Mazarazzi. Naples: (1982), pp. 577–90.

———.(Annotated edition and translation of) *Mustafa Ali's Counsel for Sultans 1581.* 2 vols. Vienna: Verlag der Österreichischen Akademie der Wissenschaften, 1979–1982.

Laiou-Thomadakis, Angeliki E. *Peasant Society in the Late Byzantine Empire.* Princeton: Princeton University Press, 1977.

Thomas, Lewis V. *A Study of Naima.* New York: New York University Press, 1972.

Tilly, Charles. "War and Peasant Rebellion in Seventeenth Century France," in Charles Tilly, *As Sociology meets History*. New York, London: Academic Press, 1984, pp. 109–44.

Veinstein, Gilles. "(Ayan) de la region d'Izmir et commerce du Levant (Deuxieme moitie du XVIIIe siecle)." *Etudes balkanique* 12.3, (1976), pp. 71–83.

Zilfi, Madeline C. *Politics of Piety: the Ottoman Ulema in Post-classical Age 1600–1800*. Minneapolis: Bibliotheca Islamica, 1988.

Index

(The index serves also as a glossary of terms)